Lectionary

Advent 2009 to the eve of Advent 2010 (Year C)

Church House Publishing

Published by Church House Publishing
Church House
Great Smith Street
London SW1P 3AZ

Telephone: 020 7898 1451
Fax: 020 7898 1449

ISBN 978-0-7151-2137-5 (standard)
978-0-7151-2138-2 (large)

Authorization

The Common Worship Calendar and Lectionaries are authorized pursuant to Canon B 2 of the Canons of the Church of England for use until further resolution of the General Synod of the Church of England.

Edited by Jonathan Goodall
Designed by Derek Birdsall & John Morgan/Omnific
Printed in England by Core Publications Ltd
Typeset by RefineCatch Ltd, Bungay, Suffolk

How to use this book

This booklet gives details of the full range of possibilities envisaged in the liturgical calendar and lectionary of *Common Worship*. Its use as a tool for the preparation of worship will require the making of several choices based first on the general celebration of the Christian year by the Church of England as a whole; second on the customary pattern of calendar in the diocese, parish and place of worship; and third on the pattern of services locally.

The **first column** comprises the Calendar of the Church with the days of the year. Observances that are mandatory are printed either in **bold** type (Sundays), in **bold** type (Principal Feasts and Holy Days) or in roman (Festivals). Optional Lesser Festivals and Commemorations are printed in ordinary roman type and *italic* type respectively.

The **second column** comprises (a) the readings and psalms for the Principal Service on Sundays, Principal Feasts and Holy Days, and Festivals, and (b) Holy Communion readings and psalms for other days of the week. On the Sundays after Trinity, the Old Testament reading and its psalm are divided into two smaller columns, indicating a choice between a 'continuous' reading week by week or a reading 'related' to the Gospel for that day.

The **third column** comprises (a) the Third Service readings and psalms for Sundays, Principal Feasts and Holy Days, and Festivals, and (b) the readings and psalms for weekday Morning Prayer.

The **fourth column** comprises (a) the Second Service readings and psalms for Sundays, Principal Feasts and Holy Days, and Festivals, and (b) the readings and psalms for weekday Evening Prayer.

Sundays, Principal Feasts and Holy Days and Festivals

Three sets of psalms and readings are provided for each Sunday, Principal Feast or Holy Day and Festival.

The **Principal Service lectionary** (based on the Revised Common Lectionary) is intended for use at the principal service of the day (whether this service is Holy Communion or some other authorized form). In most Church communities, this is likely to be the mid-morning service, but the minister is free to decide which service time normally constitutes the Principal Service of the day. This lectionary may be used twice if required – for example, at an early celebration of Holy Communion and then again at a later one.

If only **two readings** are used at the Principal Service and that service is Holy Communion, the second reading must always be the Gospel reading. When the Principal Service lectionary is used at a service other than Holy Communion, the Gospel reading need not always be chosen.

The **Second Service lectionary** is intended for a second main service. In many churches, this lectionary may be the appropriate provision for a Sunday afternoon or evening service. A Gospel reading is always provided so that this lectionary can, if necessary, be used where the second main service is a celebration of Holy Communion.

The **Third Service lectionary**, with shorter readings, is intended where a third set of psalms and readings is needed and is most appropriate for use at an office. A Gospel reading is not always provided, so this lectionary is not suitable for use at Holy Communion.

Weekdays

The Common Worship Weekday Lectionary authorized by the General Synod in 2005 comprises a lectionary (with psalms) for Holy Communion, a lectionary for Morning and Evening Prayer, and tables of psalms for Morning and Evening Prayer.

The **Daily Eucharistic Lectionary** (based on the Roman Catholic daily eucharistic lectionary) is a semi-continuous two-year lectionary with a wide use of scripture, though not complete coverage of the Bible. Two readings are provided for each day, the first from either the Old or New Testament, the second always a Gospel. Psalm provision is intended to be a brief response to the first reading. It is for use at Holy Communion normally in places with a daily or near-daily celebration with a regular congregation. It may also be used as an office lectionary.

The **lectionary for Morning and Evening Prayer** always provides two readings for each office, the first from the Old Testament and the second from the New Testament. These are generally in sequence. One of the New Testament readings for any particular day is from the Gospels.

In Ordinary Time (apart from the period from All Saints to the beginning of Advent) the **psalms for Morning and Evening Prayer** follow a sequential pattern.

In the periods from All Saints until 18 December, from the Epiphany until the Presentation of Christ in the Temple (Candlemas), from Ash Wednesday until Palm Sunday, and from the Monday after Easter Week until Pentecost, there is a choice of psalms at Morning and Evening Prayer. The psalms printed first reflect the theme of the season. Alternatively, the psalms from the Ordinary Time cycle may be used. The two sets are separated by '*or*'.

From 19 December until the Epiphany and from the Monday of Holy Week until the Saturday of Easter Week, only seasonal psalms are provided.

Where more than one psalm is given, one psalm (printed in **bold**) may be used as the sole psalm at that office.

Guidance on how these options for saying the psalms are expressed typographically can be found in the 'Notes on the Lectionary' below.

A further cycle is provided (see table on page 79), which is largely the monthly sequential cycle of psalms given in the *Book of Common Prayer*.

A single psalm for use by those who only say one office each day is provided in Prayer During the Day in *Common Worship: Daily Prayer*.

Liturgical colours

Colours are indicated by single letters: the first (always upper case) for the season or Festival; and occasionally a second (lower case) for an optional celebration on that day. Thus, for example, *Gr* for the celebration of a Lesser Festival whose liturgical colour is red, in an otherwise 'green' season.

Common of the Saints

General readings and psalms for saints' days can be found on pages 72–76; for some particular celebrations, other readings are suggested there.

Special Occasions

Readings and psalms for special occasions can be found on pages 77–78.

Notes on the Calendar 29 November 2009 — 27 November 2010

These notes are based on the Rules to Order the Christian Year (*Common Worship: Times and Seasons*, pages 24–30).

Sundays

All Sundays celebrate the paschal mystery of the death and resurrection of the Lord. They also reflect the character of the seasons in which they are set.

Principal Feasts

On these days (printed in **bold**) Holy Communion is celebrated in every cathedral and parish church, and this celebration, required by Canon B 14, may not be displaced by any other celebration, and may only be dispensed with in accordance with the provision of Canon B 14A.

Except in the case of Christmas Day and Easter Day, the celebration of the Feast *begins with Evening Prayer on the day before the Feast*, and the Collect at that Evening Prayer is that of the Feast. In the case of Christmas Eve and Easter Eve, there is proper liturgical provision (including a Collect) for the whole day.

The Epiphany may, for pastoral reasons, be celebrated on Sunday 3 January. **The Presentation of Christ in the Temple** (Candlemas) is celebrated on either Tuesday 2 February or Sunday 31 January. **All Saints' Day** may be celebrated on Sunday 31 October, replacing the Fourth Sunday before Advent.

Other Principal Holy Days

These days (printed in **bold**), and the liturgical provision for them, may not be displaced by any other celebration.

Ash Wednesday (17 February) and **Maundy Thursday** (1 April) are Principal Holy Days. On both these days Holy Communion is celebrated in every cathedral or parish church, except where there is dispensation under Canon B 14A.

Good Friday (2 April) is a Principal Holy Day.

Easter

The paschal character of **the Great Fifty Days of Easter**, from Easter Day (4 April) to Pentecost (23 May), should be celebrated throughout the season, and should not be displaced by other celebrations.

Except for a Patronal or Dedication Festival, no Festival may displace the celebration of a Sunday in Eastertide, as a memorial of the resurrection and no saint's day may be celebrated in Easter Week. The paschal character of the season should be retained on those weekdays when saints' days are celebrated.

The three days before Ascension Day (10–12 May) are customarily observed as **Rogation Days**, when prayer is offered for God's blessing on the fruits of the earth and on human labour.

The nine days **after Ascension Day until the eve of Pentecost** (14–22 May) are observed as days of prayer and preparation for the celebration of the outpouring of the Holy Spirit.

Festivals

These days (printed in roman), and the liturgical provision for them, are not usually displaced. For each day there is full liturgical provision for a Principal, Second and Third Service, and an optional so-called First Evening Prayer on the evening before the Festival where this is required.

Festivals may *not* be celebrated on Sundays in Advent, Lent or Eastertide, the Baptism of Christ, Ascension Day, Trinity Sunday or Christ the King, or weekdays between Palm Sunday and the Second Sunday of Easter. A Festival coinciding with these days is transferred to the first available day: hence in 2010 Mark the Evangelist is transferred from 25 April (the Fourth Sunday of Easter) to 26 April. Otherwise, Festivals falling on a Sunday — namely in 2009–10 John, Apostle and Evangelist (falling on the First Sunday of Christmas 2009), James the Apostle (falling on the Eighth Sunday after Trinity), the Blessed Virgin Mary (falling on the Eleventh Sunday after Trinity) and Stephen, Deacon, First Martyr (falling on the First Sunday of Christmas 2010) — may be kept on that Sunday or transferred to the Monday (or, at the discretion of the minister, to the next suitable weekday).

Certain Festivals (namely, Matthias the Apostle, the Visit of the BVM to Elizabeth, Thomas the Apostle, and the Blessed Virgin Mary) have customary alternative dates (see page 8).

The Thursday after Trinity Sunday (3 June) may be observed as the **Day of Thanksgiving for the Institution of Holy Communion** (sometimes known as *Corpus Christi*), and may be kept as a Festival.

Other Celebrations

Mothering Sunday falls on 14 March, the Fourth Sunday of Lent. Alternative prayers and readings are provided for the Principal Service.

Bible Sunday may be celebrated on 24 October, replacing the Last Sunday after Trinity, and appropriate prayers and readings are provided.

Local Celebrations

The celebration of **the patron saint or the title of a church** is kept either as a Festival or as a Principal Feast.

The **Dedication Festival** of a church is the anniversary of the date of its dedication or consecration. This is kept either as a Festival or as a Principal Feast. When kept as Principal Feasts, the Patronal and Dedication Festivals may be transferred to the nearest Sunday, unless that day is already a Principal Feast or one of the following days: the First Sunday of Advent, the Baptism of Christ, the First Sunday of Lent, the Fifth Sunday of Lent, or Palm Sunday. If the actual date is not known, the Dedication Festival may be celebrated on 3 October (replacing the Eighteenth Sunday after Trinity), or 24 October (replacing the Last Sunday after Trinity), or on a suitable date chosen locally. Readings can be found on page 71.

Harvest Thanksgiving may be celebrated on any Sunday in autumn, replacing the provision for that day, provided it does not displace any Principal Feast or Festival.

Diocesan and other local provision may be made in **the calendar of the saints** to supplement the general calendar, in accordance with Canon B 6, paragraph 5.

Lesser Festivals

Lesser Festivals (printed in ordinary roman type, in black) are observed in a manner appropriate to a particular place. Each is provided with a Collect, which may supersede the Collect of the week. For certain Lesser Festivals a complete set of eucharistic readings is provided, and for others appropriate readings may be selected from the Common of the Saints (see pages 72–76). These readings may, at the minister's discretion, supersede the Daily Eucharistic Lectionary (DEL). The weekday Psalms and Readings at Morning and Evening Prayer are not usually superseded by those for Lesser Festivals, but at the minister's discretion Psalms and Readings provided on these days for use at Holy Communion may be used instead at Morning or Evening Prayer.

The minister may be selective in the Lesser Festivals that are observed and may also keep some, or all of them, as Commemorations, perhaps especially in Advent, Lent and Easter where the character of the season ought to be sustained. If the Day of Thanksgiving for the Institution of Holy Communion (3 June) is not kept as a Festival, it may be kept as a Lesser Festival.

When a Lesser Festival falls on a Principal Feast or Holy Day, a Festival, a Sunday, or on a weekday between Palm Sunday and the Second Sunday of Easter, its celebration is normally omitted for that year. However, where there is sufficient reason, it may, at the discretion of the minister, be celebrated on the nearest available day.

Commemorations

Commemorations (printed in *italic*) are made by a mention in prayers of intercession. They are not provided with Collect, Psalm and Readings, and do not replace the usual weekday provision at Holy Communion or at Morning and Evening Prayer.

The minister may be selective in the Commemorations that are made.

Only where there is an established celebration in the wider Church or where the day has a special local significance may a Commemoration be observed as a Lesser Festival, with liturgical provision from the Common of the Saints (pages 72–76).

In designating a Commemoration as a Lesser Festival, the minister must remember the need to maintain the spirit of the season, especially of Advent, Lent and Eastertide.

Days of Discipline and Self-Denial

The weekdays of Lent and every Friday in the year are days of discipline and self-denial, with the exception of Principal Feasts, Festivals outside Lent, and Fridays from Easter Day to Pentecost. The day preceding a Principal Feast may also be appropriately kept as a day of discipline and self-denial in preparation for the Feast.

Ember Days

Ember Days should be kept, under the bishop's directions, in the week before an ordination as days of prayer for those to be ordained deacon or priest.

Ember Days may also be kept even when there is no ordination in the diocese as more general days of prayer for those who serve the Church in its various ministries, both ordained and lay, and for vocations. Traditionally they have been observed on the Wednesday, Friday and Saturday in the week before the Third Sunday of Advent, the Second Sunday of Lent, and the Sundays nearest to 29 June and 29 September.

Ordinary Time

Ordinary Time comprises two periods in the year: first, the period from the day after the Presentation of Christ in the Temple until the day before Ash Wednesday, and second, that from the day after Pentecost until the day before the First Sunday of Advent.

During Ordinary Time, there is no seasonal emphasis, except that the period between All Saints' Day and the First Sunday of Advent is observed as a time to celebrate and reflect upon the reign of Christ in earth and heaven.

Liturgical Colours

Appropriate liturgical colours are suggested in this booklet. They are not mandatory; traditional or local use may be followed.

Notes on the Lectionary

The Sunday and festal readings for the First Sunday of Advent 2009 to 27 November 2010 (the eve of Advent) are from **Year C**, which offers a semi-continuous reading of Luke's Gospel at the Principal Service on Sundays throughout the year.

The weekday readings for Holy Communion are from **Year Two** of the Daily Eucharistic Lectionary (DEL).

Office readings are from Table 2 of the Weekday Lectionary: at Morning Prayer, Old Testament 1 and New Testament 2; and at Evening Prayer, Old Testament 2 and New Testament 2.

All **Bible references** (except to the Psalms) are to the *New Revised Standard Version* (New York, 1989). Those who use other Bible translations should check the verse numbers against the *NRSV*. Each reference gives book, chapter and verse, in that order.

References to the psalms are to the Common Worship psalter, published in *Common Worship: Services and Prayers for the Church of England* (2000) and *Common Worship: Daily Prayer* (2005). A table showing the verse number differences between this and the psalter in the *Book of Common Prayer* is provided on the Common Worship web site (http://www.cofe.anglican.org/commonworship).

Options in the provision of readings or psalms are presented in the following ways:

¶ square brackets [xx] give either optional additional verses or psalms, or a shorter alternative;

¶ '*or*' indicates a simple choice between two alternative readings or courses of psalms;

¶ a psalm printed in **bold** may be used as the sole psalm at that office;

¶ on weekdays a psalm printed in parentheses (xx) is omitted if it has been used as the opening canticle at that office;

¶ a psalm marked with an asterisk may be shortened if desired.

Where a reading from the **Apocrypha** is offered, an alternative Old Testament reading is provided.

In the choice of **readings other than the Gospel** reading, the minister should ensure that, in any year, a balance is maintained between readings from the Old and New Testaments and that, where a particular biblical book is appointed to be read over several weeks, the choice ensures that the continuity of one book is not lost.

On the Sundays after Trinity, the Principal Service Lectionary provides **alternative Old Testament readings and psalms**. References in the left-hand column (under the heading 'Continuous') offer a *semi-continuous* reading of Old Testament texts. Such a reading and its complementary psalmody stand independently of the other readings. References in the right-hand column (under the heading 'Related') *relate* the Old Testament reading and the psalm to the Gospel reading. One column should be followed for the whole sequence of Sundays after Trinity.

Notes on Collects

For a table showing where the Collects and Post Communions are published, see page 71.

Where a Collect ends 'through Jesus Christ . . . now and for ever', the minister may omit the longer (trinitarian) ending and use the shorter ending, 'through Jesus Christ our Lord', to which the people respond, 'Amen'. The longer ending, however, is to be preferred at a service of Holy Communion.

The Collect for each Sunday is used at Evening Prayer on the Saturday preceding, except where that Saturday is a Principal Feast, or a Festival, or the eve of Christmas Day or Easter Day. The Collect for each Sunday is also used on the weekdays following, except where other provision is made.

Abbreviations used in this book

Alt	Alternative
Bp	Bishop
BVM	Blessed Virgin Mary
Cant	Canticle
Comps	Companions
DEL	Daily Eucharistic Lectionary
EP	Evening Prayer
G	Green
HC	Holy Communion: *used where additional references are given to provide alternative texts for use at a celebration of Holy Communion (most often the provision of a psalm or gospel)*
Mm	Martyrs
MP	Morning Prayer
P or p	Purple or Violet
P(La)	Purple or Lent Array
Ps & Pss	Psalmody
R or r	Red
Ss	Saints
vv	Verses: used where the source is not subdivided into chapters
W or w	White (Gold is indicated where its use would be appropriate)
Eccles	Ecclesiastes
Ecclus	Ecclesiasticus
Sol	Song of Solomon (also called Song of Songs)

Standard abbreviations have been used for other books of the Bible where necessary.

Alternative dates

The following may be celebrated on the alternative dates indicated:

Chad
– with Cedd on 26 October instead of 2 March

Cuthbert
– on 4 September instead of 20 March

Matthias the Apostle
– on 24 February instead of 14 May

The Visit of the Blessed Virgin Mary to Elizabeth
– on 2 July instead of 31 May

Thomas the Apostle
– on 21 December instead of 3 July

The Blessed Virgin Mary
– on 8 September instead of 15 August

Thomas Becket
– on 7 July instead of 29 December

If any of these three festivals is celebrated on the alternative date these provisions should be used on the principal date:

Holy Communion	Morning Prayer	Evening Prayer
If Matthias the Apostle is celebrated on Tuesday 24 February the following provision is used on Thursday 14 May (W):		
Acts 18.9–18	Psalms 20, **81** *or* **88** (95)	Psalm **145** *or* **102**
Psalm 47.1–6	Numbers 20.1–13	Deuteronomy 29.2–15
John 16.20–23	Luke 7.11–17	1 John 1.1—2.6
		**Exodus 35.30—36.1; Galatians 5.13–end*
If the Visit of the Blessed Virgin Mary to Elizabeth is celebrated on Friday 2 July the following provision is used on Monday 31 May (G):		
2 Peter 1.2–7	Psalms **1**, 2, 3	Psalms **4**, 7
Psalm 91.1–2, 14–end	Joshua 7.1–15	2 Chronicles 26.1–21
Mark 12.1–12	Luke 10.25–37	Romans 4.1–12
If Thomas the Apostle is celebrated on Monday 21 December the following provision is used on Friday 3 July (G):		
Amos 9.11–end	Psalms 96, **97**, 100	Psalm **104**
Psalm 85.8–end	Judges 18.1–20, 27–end	Nehemiah 9.24–end
Matthew 9.14–17	Luke 19.11–27	Romans 16.17–end

Key to the Tables

For guidance on how the options for saying the psalms are expressed typographically, see page 7.

Sundays (and Principal Feasts, other Principal Holy Days, and Festivals)

			Principal Service	3rd Service	2nd Service
Day	**Date** **Sunday / Feast** † / Festival ††	*Colour*	Main service of the day: Holy Communion, Morning Prayer, Evening Prayer, or a Service of the Word	Shorter Readings, an Office lectionary probably used at Morning Prayer where Holy Communion is the Principal Service	2nd main Service, probably used at Evening Prayer; adaptable for Holy Communion

† Principal Feasts and other Principal Holy Days are printed in **bold**.
†† Festivals are printed in roman typeface.

Weekdays

			Holy Communion	Morning Prayer	Evening Prayer
Day	**Date** Lesser Festival ‡* [optional] *Commemoration* ‡‡ [optional]	*Colour*	Weekday readings	Psalms and readings for Morning Prayer	Psalms and readings for Evening Prayer

‡ Lesser Festivals are printed in roman typeface, in black.
‡‡ Commemorations are printed in *italics*.
* The ascriptions given to holy men and women in the Calendar (such as martyr, teacher of the faith, etc.) have often been abbreviated in this booklet for reasons of space. The particular ascription given is there to be helpful if needing to choose Collects and readings from Common of the Saints; where several ascriptions are used (e.g. bishop and martyr), traditionally the last ascription given is the most important and therefore the guiding one. The full ascriptions may be found in the Calendar, which is printed in *Common Worship: Times and Seasons* (pages 7–22), *Common Worship: Festivals* (pages 5–20) and *Common Worship: Daily Prayer* (pages 5–16). These incorporate minor corrections made since the publication of the Calendar in *Common Worship: Services and Prayers for the Church of England* (pages 5–16).

Advent 1

		Principal Service	3rd Service	2nd Service
Sunday	**29 November** *P* **1st Sunday of Advent**	Jeremiah 33.14–16 Psalm 25.1–9 1 Thessalonians 3.9–end Luke 21.25–36	Psalm 44 Isaiah 51.4–11 Romans 13.11–end	Psalm 9 [9.1–8] Joel 3.9–end Revelation 14.13—15.4 *HC* John 3.1–17 *or:* 1st EP of Andrew the Apostle: Psalm 48; Isaiah 49.1–9*a*; 1 Corinthians 4.9–16
Monday	**30 November** *R* Andrew the Apostle	Isaiah 52.7–10 Psalm 19.1–6 Romans 10.12–18 Matthew 4.18–22	*MP* Psalms 47, 147.1–12 Ezekiel 47.1–12 *or* Ecclesiasticus 14.20–end John 12.20–32	*EP* Psalms 87, 96 Zechariah 8.20–end John 1.35–42
		Holy Communion	**Morning Prayer**	**Evening Prayer**
Tuesday	**1 December** *P* *Charles de Foucauld, hermit, 1916*	Isaiah 11.1–10 Psalm 72.1–4, 18–19 Luke 10.21–24	Psalms **80**, 82 *or* **5**, 6 (8) Isaiah 26.1–13 Matthew 12.22–37	Psalms **74**, 75 *or* **9**, 10* Isaiah 43.1–13 Revelation 20
Wednesday	**2 December** *P*	Isaiah 25.6–10*a* Psalm 23 Matthew 15.29–37	Psalms 5, **7** *or* **119.1–32** Isaiah 28.1–13 Matthew 12.38–end	Psalms 76, **77** *or* **11**, 12, 13 Isaiah 43.14–end Revelation 21.1–8
Thursday	**3 December** *P* *Francis Xavier, missionary, 1552*	Isaiah 26.1–6 Psalm 118.18–27*a* Matthew 7.21, 24–27	Psalms **42**, 43 *or* 14, **15**, 16 Isaiah 28.14–end Matthew 13.1–23	Psalms **40**, 46 *or* **18*** Isaiah 44.1–8 Revelation 21.9–21
Friday	**4 December** *P* *John of Damascus, monk, teacher of the faith, c.749* *Nicholas Ferrar, deacon, founder of the Little Gidding community, 1637*	Isaiah 29.17–end Psalm 27.1–4, 16–17 Matthew 9.27–31	Psalms **25**, 26 *or* 17, **19** Isaiah 29.1–14 Matthew 13.24–43	Psalms 16, **17** *or* **22** Isaiah 44.9–23 Revelation 21.22—22.5
Saturday	**5 December** *P*	Isaiah 30.19–21, 23–26 Psalm 146.4–9 Matthew 9.35—10.1, 6–8	Psalms **9** (10) *or* 20, 21, **23** Isaiah 29.15–end Matthew 13.44–end	Psalms **27**, 28 *or* **24**, 25 Isaiah 44.24—45.13 Revelation 22.6–end

			Principal Service	3rd Service	2nd Service
Sunday	**6 December** **2nd Sunday of Advent**	*P*	Baruch 5 *or* Malachi 3.1–4 *Canticle:* Benedictus Philippians 1.3–11 Luke 3.1–6	Psalm 80 Isaiah 64.1–7 Matthew 11.2–11	Psalms 75 [76] Isaiah 40.1–11 Luke 1.1–25
			Holy Communion	**Morning Prayer**	**Evening Prayer**
Monday	**7 December** Ambrose, bishop, teacher of the faith, 397 (see p. 74)	*Pw*	Isaiah 35 Psalm 85.7–end Luke 5.17–26	Psalms **44** *or* 27, **30** Isaiah 30.1–18 Matthew 14.1–12	Psalms **144**, 146 *or* 26, **28**, 29 Isaiah 45.14–end 1 Thessalonians 1
Tuesday	**8 December** Conception of the Blessed Virgin Mary (see p. 72)	*Pw*	Isaiah 40.1–11 Psalm 96.1, 10–end Matthew 18.12–14	Psalms **56**, 57 *or* 32, **36** Isaiah 30.19–end Matthew 14.13–end	Psalms **11**, 12, 13 *or* **33** Isaiah 46 1 Thessalonians 2.1–12
Wednesday	**9 December** Ember Day	*P*	Isaiah 40.25–end Psalm 103.8–13 Matthew 11.28–end	Psalms **62**, 63 *or* **34** Isaiah 31 Matthew 15.1–20	Psalms **10**, 14 *or* **119.33–56** Isaiah 47 1 Thessalonians 2.13–end
Thursday	**10 December**	*P*	Isaiah 41.13–20 Psalm 145.1, 8–13 Matthew 11.11–15	Psalms 53, **54**, 60 *or* **37*** Isaiah 32 Matthew 15.21–28	Psalms **73** *or* 39, **40** Isaiah 48.1–11 1 Thessalonians 3
Friday	**11 December** Ember Day	*P*	Isaiah 48.17–19 Psalm 1 Matthew 11.16–19	Psalms 85, **86** *or* **31** Isaiah 33.1–22 Matthew 15.29–end	Psalms 82, **90** *or* **35** Isaiah 48.12–end 1 Thessalonians 4.1–12
Saturday	**12 December** Ember Day	*P*	Ecclesiasticus 48.1–4, 9–11 *or* 2 Kings 2.9–12 Psalm 80.1–4, 18–19 Matthew 17.10–13	Psalms **145** *or* 41, **42**, 43 Isaiah 35 Matthew 16.1–12	Psalms 93, **94** *or* 45, **46** Isaiah 49.1–13 1 Thessalonians 4.13–end

Advent 3

		Principal Service	3rd Service	2nd Service
Sunday	**13 December** *P* **3rd Sunday of Advent**	Zephaniah 3.14–end *Canticle:* Isaiah 12.2–end *or* Psalm 146.4–10 Philippians 4.4–7 Luke 3.7–18	Psalms 12, 14 Isaiah 25.1–9 1 Corinthians 4.1–5	Psalms 50.1–6 [62] Isaiah 35 Luke 1.57–66 [67–end]
		Holy Communion	**Morning Prayer**	**Evening Prayer**
Monday	**14 December** *Pw* John of the Cross, poet, teacher of the faith, 1591 (see p. 73)	Numbers 24.2–7, 15–17 Psalm 25.3–8 Matthew 21.23–27	Psalms **40** *or* **44** Isaiah 38. 1–8, 21–22 Matthew 16.13–end	Psalms 25, **26** *or* **47**, 49 Isaiah 49.14–25 1 Thessalonians 5.1–11
Tuesday	**15 December** *P*	Zephaniah 3.1–2, 9–13 Psalm 34.1–6, 21–22 Matthew 21.28–32	Psalms **70**, 74 *or* **48**, 52 Isaiah 38. 9–20 Matthew 17.1–13	Psalms **50**, 54 *or* **50** Isaiah 50 1 Thessalonians 5.12–end
Wednesday	**16 December** *P*	Isaiah 45.6*b*–8, 18, 21*b*–end Psalm 85.7–end Luke 7.18*b*–23	Psalms **75**, 96 *or* **119.57–80** Isaiah 39 Matthew 17.14–21	Psalms 25, **82** *or* **59**, 60 (67) Isaiah 51.1–8 2 Thessalonians 1
Thursday	**17 December** *P* *O Sapientia* *Eglantyne Jebb, social reformer, founder of 'Save The Children', 1928*	Genesis 49.2, 8–10 Psalm 72.1–5, 18–19 Matthew 1.1–17	Psalms **76**, 97 *or* 56, **57** (63*) Zephaniah 1.1—2.3 Matthew 17.22–end	Psalms **44** *or* 61, **62**, 64 Isaiah 51.9–16 2 Thessalonians 2
Friday	**18 December** *P*	Jeremiah 23.5–8 Psalm 72. 1–2, 12–13, 18–end Matthew 1.18–24	Psalms 77, **98** *or* **51**, 54 Zephaniah 3.1–13 Matthew 18.1–20	Psalm **49** *or* **38** Isaiah 51.17–end 2 Thessalonians 3
			From 19 December until the Epiphany the seasonal psalmody must be used at Morning and Evening Prayer.	
Saturday	**19 December** *P*	Judges 13.2–7, 24–end Psalm 71.3–8 Luke 1.5–25	Psalms 144, **146** Zephaniah 3.14–end Matthew 18.21–end	Psalms 10, **57** Isaiah 52.1–12 Jude

			Principal Service	3rd Service	2nd Service
Sunday	**20 December** **4th Sunday of Advent**	*P*	Micah 5.2–5*a* *Canticle:* Magnificat *or* Psalm 80.1–8 Hebrews 10.5–10 Luke 1.39–45[46–55]	Psalm 144 Isaiah 32.1–8 Revelation 22.6–end	Psalms 123 [131] Isaiah 10.33—11.10 Matthew 1.18–end
			Holy Communion	**Morning Prayer**	**Evening Prayer**
Monday	**21 December**	*P*	Zephaniah 3.14–18 Psalm 33.1–4, 11–12, 20–end Luke 1.39–45	Psalms **121**, 122, 123 Malachi 1.1, 6–end Matthew 19.1–12	Psalms 80, **84** Isaiah 52.13—end of 53 2 Peter 1.1–15
Tuesday	**22 December**	*P*	1 Samuel 1.24–end Psalm 113 Luke 1.46–56	Psalms **124**, 125, 126, 127 Malachi 2.1–16 Matthew 19.13–15	Psalms 24, **48** Isaiah 54 2 Peter 1.16—2.3
Wednesday	**23 December**	*P*	Malachi 3.1–4, 4.5–end Psalm 25.3–9 Luke 1.57–66	Psalms 128, 129, **130**, 131 Malachi 2.17—3.12 Matthew 19.16–end	Psalm **89.1–37** Isaiah 55 2 Peter 2.4–end
Thursday	**24 December** **Christmas Eve**	*P*	*Morning Eucharist only:* 2 Samuel 7.1–5, 8–11, 16 Psalm 89.2, 19–27 Acts 13.16–26 Luke 1.67–79	Psalms **45**, 113 Malachi 3.13—end of 4 Matthew 23.1–12	Psalm **85** Zechariah 2 Revelation 1.1–8
			Principal Service	**3rd Service**	**2nd Service**
Friday	**25 December** **Christmas Day**		*Gold or W* *Any of the following three sets of Principal Service readings may be used on the evening of Christmas Eve and on Christmas Day. Set III should be used at some point during the celebration.* **Set I**: Isaiah 9.2–7; Psalm 96; Titus 2.11–14; Luke 2.1–14 [15–20] **Set II**: Isaiah 62.6–end; Psalm 97; Titus 3.4–7; Luke 2. [1–7] 8–20 **Set III**: Isaiah 52.7–10; Psalm 98; Hebrews 1.1–4 [5–12]; John 1.1–14	*MP* Psalms **110**, 117 Isaiah 62.1–5 Matthew 1.18–end	*EP* Psalm 8 Isaiah 65.17–25 Philippians 2.5–11 *or* Luke 2.1–20 *if it has not been used at the principal service of the day*
Saturday	**26 December** Stephen, deacon, first martyr	*R*	2 Chronicles 24.20–22 *or* Acts 7.51–end Psalm 119.161–168 Acts 7.51–end *or* Galatians 2.16*b*–20 Matthew 10.17–22	*MP* Psalms **13**, 31.1–8, 150 Jeremiah 26.12–15 Acts 6	*EP* Psalms 57, **86** Genesis 4.1–10 Matthew 23.34–end

John / Christmas 1

If John is celebrated on Sunday 27 December:

		Principal Service	3rd Service	2nd Service
Sunday	**27 December** *W* John, Apostle and Evangelist	Exodus 33.7–11*a* Psalm 117 1 John 1 John 21.19*b*–end	*MP* Psalms **21**, 147.13–end Exodus 33.12–end 1 John 2.1–11	*EP* Psalm **97** Isaiah 6.1–8 1 John 5.1–12
Monday	**28 December** *R* The Holy Innocents	Jeremiah 31.15–17 Psalm 124 1 Corinthians 1.26–29 Matthew 2.13–18	*MP* Psalms **36**, 146 Baruch 4.21–27 *or* Genesis 37.13–20 Matthew 18.1–10	*EP* Psalms 123, **128** Isaiah 49.14–25 Mark 10.13–16
		Holy Communion	**Morning Prayer**	**Evening Prayer**
Tuesday	**29 December** *Wr* Thomas Becket, archbishop, martyr, 1170 (see p. 72)	1 John 2.3–11 Psalm 96.1–4 Luke 2.22–35	Psalms **19**, 20 Jonah 1 Colossians 1.1–14	Psalms 131, **132** Isaiah 57.15–end John 1.1–18

If John is celebrated on Tuesday 29 December:

		Principal Service	3rd Service	2nd Service
Sunday	**27 December** *W* **1st Sunday of Christmas**	1 Samuel 2.18–20, 26 Psalm 148 [148.7–end] Colossians 3.12–17 Luke 2.41–end	Psalm 105.1–11 Isaiah 41.21—42.1 1 John 1.1–7	Psalm 132 Isaiah 61 Galatians 3.27—4.7 *HC* Luke 2.15–21
		Holy Communion	**Morning Prayer**	**Evening Prayer**
Monday	**28 December** *R* The Holy Innocents	Jeremiah 31.15–17 Psalm 124 1 Corinthians 1.26–29 Matthew 2.13–18	*MP* Psalms **36**, 146 Baruch 4.21–27 *or* Genesis 37.13–20 Matthew 18.1–10	*EP* Psalms 123, **128** Isaiah 49.14–25 Mark 10.13–16
Tuesday	**29 December** *W* John, Apostle and Evangelist	Exodus 33.7–11*a* Psalm 117 1 John 1 John 21.19*b*–end	*MP* Psalms **21**, 147.13–end Exodus 33.12–end 1 John 2.1–11	*EP* Psalm **97** Isaiah 6.1–8 1 John 5.1–12

			Holy Communion	Morning Prayer	Evening Prayer
Wednesday	**30 December**	*W*	1 John 2.12–17 Psalm 96.7–10 Luke 2.36–40	Psalms 111, 112, **113** Jonah 2 Colossians 1.15–23	Psalms **65**, 84 Isaiah 59.1–15*a* John 1.19–28
Thursday	**31 December** *John Wyclif, reformer, 1384*	*W*	1 John 2.18–21 Psalm 96.1, 11–end John 1.1–18	Psalm **102** Jonah 3–4 Colossians 1.24—2.7	Psalms **90**, 148 Isaiah 59.15*b*–end John 1.29–34 *or:* 1st EP of the Naming and Circumcision of Jesus: Psalm 148; Jeremiah 23.1–6; Colossians 2.8–15
			Principal Service	**3rd Service**	**2nd Service**
Friday	**1 January** Naming and Circumcision of Jesus	*W*	Numbers 6.22–end Psalm 8 Galatians 4.4–7 Luke 2.15–21	*MP* Psalms **103**, 150 Genesis 17.1–13 Romans 2.17–end	*EP* Psalm **115** Deuteronomy 30. [1–10] 11–end Acts 3.1–16
			Holy Communion	**Morning Prayer**	**Evening Prayer**
Saturday	**2 January** Basil the Great and Gregory of Nazianzus, bishops, teachers of the faith, 379 and 389 (see p. 73) *Seraphim, monk, spiritual guide, 1833* *Vedanayagam Samuel Azariah, bishop, evangelist, 1945*	*W*	1 John 2.22–28 Psalm 98.1–4 John 1.19–28	Psalm **18.1–30** Ruth 1 Colossians 2.8–end	Psalms 45, **46** Isaiah 60.1–12 John 1.35–42 *or, if the Epiphany is celebrated on Sunday 3 January:* **1st EP of the Epiphany:** Psalms 96, **97;** Isaiah 49.1–13; John 4.7–26

Christmas 2 / Epiphany

If the Epiphany is celebrated on Wednesday 6 January:

			Principal Service	3rd Service	2nd Service
Sunday	**3 January** **2nd Sunday of Christmas**	*W*	Jeremiah 31.7–14 Psalm 147.13–end Ecclesiasticus 24.1–12 *Canticle:* Wisdom of Solomon 10.15–end Ephesians 1.3–14 John 1.[1–9] 10–18	Psalm 87 Isaiah 12 1 Thessalonians 2.1–8	Psalm 135 [135.1–14] 1 Samuel 1.20–end 1 John 4.7–16 *HC* Matthew 2.13–end

			Holy Communion	Morning Prayer	Evening Prayer
Monday	**4 January**	*W*	1 John 3.7–10 Psalm 98.1, 8–end John 1.35–42	Psalm **89.1–37** Ruth 3 Colossians 3.12—4.1	Psalms 85, **87** Isaiah 61 John 2.1–12
Tuesday	**5 January**	*W*	1 John 3.11–21 Psalm 100 John 1.43–end	Psalms 8, **48** Ruth 4.1–17 Colossians 4.2–end	**1st EP of the Epiphany:** Psalms 96, **97** Isaiah 49.1–13 John 4.7–26

			Principal Service	3rd Service	2nd Service
Wednesday	**6 January** **Epiphany**	*Gold or W*	Isaiah 60.1–6 Psalm 72. [1–9] 10–15 Ephesians 3.1–12 Matthew 2.1–12	*MP* Psalms **132**, 113 Jeremiah 31.7–14 John 1.29–34	*EP* Psalms **98**, 100 Baruch 4.36—end of 5 *or* Isaiah 60.1–9 John 2.1–11

			Holy Communion	Morning Prayer	Evening Prayer
Thursday	**7 January**	*W*	1 John 3.22—4.6 Psalm 2.7–end Matthew 4.12–17, 23–end	Psalms **99**, 147.1–12 *or* **78.1–39*** Baruch 1.15—2.10 *or* Jeremiah 23.1–8 Matthew 20.1–16	Psalms **118** *or* **78.40–end*** Isaiah 63.7–end 1 John 3
Friday	**8 January**	*W*	1 John 4.7–10 Psalm 72.1–8 Mark 6.34–44	Psalms **46**, 147.13–end *or* **55** Baruch 2.11–end *or* Jeremiah 30.1–17 Matthew 20.17–28	Psalms **145** *or* **69** Isaiah 64 1 John 4.7–end
Saturday	**9 January**	*W*	1 John 4.11–18 Psalm 72.1, 10–13 Mark 6.45–52	Psalms 2, **148** *or* **76**, 79 Baruch 3.1–8 *or* Jeremiah 30.18—31.9 Matthew 20.29–end	Psalms **67**, 72 *or* 81, **84** Isaiah 65.1–16 1 John 5.1–12

Epiphany

If the Epiphany is celebrated on Sunday 3 January:

			Principal Service	3rd Service	2nd Service
Sunday	**3 January** **Epiphany**	*Gold or W*	Isaiah 60.1–6 Psalm 72. [1–9] 10–15 Ephesians 3.1–12 Matthew 2.1–12	*MP* Psalms **132**, 113 Jeremiah 31.7–14 John 1.29–34	*EP* Psalms **98**, 100 Baruch 4.36—end of 5 *or* Isaiah 60.1–9 John 2.1–11
			Holy Communion	**Morning Prayer**	**Evening Prayer**
Monday	**4 January**	W	I John 3.22—4.6 Psalm 2.7–end Matthew 4.12–17, 23–end	Psalms **89.1–37** *or* **71** Ruth 2 Colossians 3.1–11	Psalms 85, **87** *or* **72**, 75 Isaiah 60.13–end John 1.43–end
Tuesday	**5 January**	W	I John 4.7–10 Psalm 72.1–8 Mark 6.34–44	Psalms 8, **48** *or* **73** Ruth 3 Colossians 3.12—4.1	Psalms 96, **97** *or* **74** Isaiah 61 John 2.1–12
Wednesday	**6 January**	W	I John 4.11–18 Psalm 72.1, 10–13 Mark 6.45–52	Psalms **127**, 128, 131 *or* **77** Ruth 4.1–17 Colossians 4.2–end	Psalms **2**, 110 *or* **119.81–104** Isaiah 62 John 2.13–end
Thursday	**7 January**	W	I John 4.19—5.4 Psalm 72.1, 17–end Luke 4.14–22	Psalms **99**, 147.1–12 *or* **78.1–39*** Baruch 1.15—2.10 *or* Jeremiah 23.1–8	Psalms **118** *or* **78.40–end*** Isaiah 63.7–end
Friday	**8 January**	W	I John 5.5–13 Psalm 147.13–end Luke 5.12–16	Psalms **46**, 147.13–end *or* **55** Baruch 2.11–end *or* Jeremiah 30.1–17 Matthew 20.17–28	Psalms **145** *or* **69** Isaiah 64 I John 4.7–end
Saturday	**9 January**	W	I John 5.14–end Psalm 149.1–5 John 3.22–30	Psalms 2, **148** *or* **76**, 79 Baruch 3.1–8 *or* Jeremiah 30.18—31.9 Matthew 20.29–end	Psalms **67**, 72 *or* 81, **84** Isaiah 65.1–16 I John 5.1–12 *or:* 1st EP of the Baptism of Christ: Psalm 36; Isaiah 61; Titus 2.11–14; 3.4–7

Baptism of Christ / Epiphany 1

			Principal Service	3rd Service	2nd Service
Sunday	**10 January** The Baptism of Christ *1st Sunday of Epiphany*	*Gold or W*	Isaiah 43.1–7 Psalm 29 Acts 8.14–17 Luke 3.15–17, 21–22	Psalm 89.19–29 Isaiah 42.1–9 Acts 19.1–7	Psalms 46, 47 Isaiah 55.1–11 Romans 6.1–11 *HC* Mark 1.4–11
			Holy Communion	**Morning Prayer**	**Evening Prayer**
Monday	**11 January** *Mary Slessor, missionary, 1915* DEL week 1	W	1 Samuel 1.1–8 Psalm 116.10–15 Mark 1.14–20	Psalms **2**, 110 *or* **80**, 82 Genesis 1.1–19 Matthew 21.1–17	Psalms **34**, 36 *or* **85**, 86 Amos 1 1 Corinthians 1.1–17
Tuesday	**12 January** Aelred, abbot, 1167 (see p. 75) *Benedict Biscop, scholar, 689*	W	1 Samuel 1.9–20 *Canticle:* 1 Samuel 2.1, 4–8 *or* Magnificat Mark 1.21–28	Psalms 8, **9** *or* 87, **89.1–18** Genesis 1.20—2.3 Matthew 21.18–32	Psalms **45**, 46 *or* **89.19–end** Amos 2 1 Corinthians 1.18–end
Wednesday	**13 January** Hilary, bishop, teacher of the faith, 367 (see p. 73) *Kentigern (Mungo), missionary bishop, 603* *George Fox, founder of the Society of Friends (Quakers), 1691*	W	1 Samuel 3.1–10, 19–20 Psalm 40.1–4, 7–10 Mark 1.29–39	Psalms 19, **20** *or* **119.105–128** Genesis 2.4–end Matthew 21.33–end	Psalms **47**, 48 *or* **91**, 93 Amos 3 1 Corinthians 2
Thursday	**14 January**	W	1 Samuel 4.1–11 Psalm 44.10–15, 24–25 Mark 1.40–end	Psalms **21**, 24 *or* 90, **92** Genesis 3 Matthew 22.1–14	Psalms **61**, 65 *or* **94** Amos 4 1 Corinthians 3
Friday	**15 January**	W	1 Samuel 8.4–7, 10–end Psalm 89.15–18 Mark 2.1–12	Psalms **67**, 72 *or* **88** (95) Genesis 4.1–16, 25–26 Matthew 22.15–33	Psalm **68** *or* **102** Amos 5.1–17 1 Corinthians 4
Saturday	**16 January**	W	1 Samuel 9.1–4, 17–19, 10.1*a* Psalm 21.1–6 Mark 2.13–17	Psalms 29, **33** *or* 96, **97**, 100 Genesis 6.1–10 Matthew 22.34–end	Psalms 84, **85** *or* **104** Amos 5.18–end 1 Corinthians 5

		Principal Service	**3rd Service**	**2nd Service**
Sunday	**17 January** *W* **2nd Sunday of Epiphany**	Isaiah 62.1–5 Psalm 36.5–10 1 Corinthians 12.1–11 John 2.1–11	Psalm 145.1–13 Isaiah 49.1–7 Acts 16.11–15	Psalm 96 1 Samuel 3.1–20 Ephesians 4.1–16 *HC* John 1.29–42
		Holy Communion	**Morning Prayer**	**Evening Prayer**
Monday	**18 January** *W* DEL week 2 ***Week of Prayer for Christian Unity: 18–25 January***	1 Samuel 15.16–23 Psalm 50.8–10, 16–17, 24 Mark 2.18–22	Psalms 145, **146** *or* **98**, 99, 101 Genesis 6.11—7.10 Matthew 24.1–14	Psalms **71** *or* **105*** (*or* 103) Amos 6 1 Corinthians 6.1–11
Tuesday	**19 January** *W* Wulfstan, bishop, 1095 (see p. 74)	1 Samuel 16.1–13 Psalm 89.19–27 Mark 2.23–end	Psalms **132**, 147.1–12 *or* **106*** (*or* 103) Genesis 7.11–end Matthew 24.15–28	Psalms **89.1–37** *or* **107*** Amos 7 1 Corinthians 6.12–end
Wednesday	**20 January** *W* *Richard Rolle, spiritual writer, 1349*	1 Samuel 17.32–33, 37, 40–51 Psalm 144.1–2, 9–10 Mark 3.1–6	Psalms **81**, 147.13–end *or* 110, **111**, 112 Genesis 8.1–14 Matthew 24.29–end	Psalms **97**, 98 *or* **119.129–152** Amos 8 1 Corinthians 7.1–24
Thursday	**21 January** *Wr* Agnes, child martyr, 304 (see p. 72)	1 Samuel 18.6–9, 19.1–7 Psalm 56.1–2, 8–end Mark 3.7–12	Psalms **76**, 148 *or* 113, **115** Genesis 8.15—9.7 Matthew 25.1–13	Psalms 99, 100, **111** *or* 114, **116**, 117 Amos 9 1 Corinthians 7.25–end
Friday	**22 January** *W* *Vincent of Saragossa, deacon, martyr, 304*	1 Samuel 24.3–22a Psalm 57.1–2, 8–end Mark 3.13–19	Psalms **27**, 149 *or* **139** Genesis 9.8–19 Matthew 25.14–30	Psalms **73** *or* **130**, 131, 137 Hosea 1.1—2.1 1 Corinthians 8
Saturday	**23 January** *W*	2 Samuel 1.1–4, 11–12, 17–19, 23–end Psalm 80.1–6 Mark 3.20–21	Psalms **122**, 128, 150 *or* 120, **121**, 122 Genesis 11.1–9 Matthew 25.31–end	Psalms **61**, 66 *or* **118** Hosea 2.2–17 1 Corinthians 9.1–14

Epiphany 3

		Principal Service	3rd Service	2nd Service
Sunday	**24 January** *W* **3rd Sunday of Epiphany**	Nehemiah 8.1–3, 5–6, 8–10 Psalm 19 [*or* 19.1–6] 1 Corinthians 12.12–31*a* Luke 4.14–21	Psalm 113 Deuteronomy 30.11–15 3 John 1, 5–8	Psalm 33 [*or* 33.1–12] Numbers 9.15–end 1 Corinthians 7.17–24 *HC* Mark 1.21–28 *or:* 1st EP of the Conversion of Paul: Psalm 149; Isaiah 49.1–13; Acts 22.3–16
Monday	**25 January** *W* Conversion of Paul	Jeremiah 1.4–10 *or* Acts 9.1–22 Psalm 67 Acts 9.1–22 *or* Galatians 1.11–16*a* Matthew 19.27–end	*MP* Psalms 66, 147.13–end Ezekiel 3.22–end Philippians 3.1–14	*EP* Psalm 119.41–56 Ecclesiasticus 39.1–10 *or* Isaiah 56.1–8 Colossians 1.24—2.7
		Holy Communion	**Morning Prayer**	**Evening Prayer**
Tuesday	**26 January** *W* Timothy and Titus, companions of Paul DEL week 3	2 Samuel 6.12–15, 17–19 Psalm 24.7–end Mark 3.31–end *Lesser Festival eucharistic lectionary:* Isaiah 61.1–3*a*; Psalm 100; 2 Timothy 2.1–8 *or* Titus 1.1–5; Luke 10.1–9	Psalms 34, **36** *or* **132**, 133 Genesis 13.2–end Matthew 26.17–35	Psalms **145** *or* (134,) **135** Hosea 4.1–16 1 Corinthians 10.1–13
Wednesday	**27 January** *W*	2 Samuel 7.4–17 Psalm 89.19–27 Mark 4.1–20	Psalms 45, **46** *or* **119.153–end** Genesis 14 Matthew 26.36–46	Psalms 21, **29** *or* **136** Hosea 5.1–7 1 Corinthians 10.14—11.1
Thursday	**28 January** *W* Thomas Aquinas, priest, philosopher, teacher of the faith, 1274 (see p. 73)	2 Samuel 7.18–19, 24–end Psalm 132.1–5, 11–15 Mark 4.21–25	Psalms **47**, 48 *or* **143**, 146 Genesis 15 Matthew 26.47–56	Psalms **24**, 33 *or* **138**, 140, 141 Hosea 5.8—6.6 1 Corinthians 11.2–16
Friday	**29 January** *W*	2 Samuel 11.1–10, 13–17 Psalm 51.1–6, 9 Mark 4.26–34	Psalms 61, **65** *or* 142, **144** Genesis 16 Matthew 26.57–end	Psalms **67**, 77 *or* **145** Hosea 6.7—7.2 1 Corinthians 11.17–end
Saturday	**30 January** *Wr* Charles, king and martyr, 1649 (see p. 72)	2 Samuel 12.1–7, 10–17 Psalm 51.11–16 Mark 4.35–end	Psalms **68** *or* **147** Genesis 17.1–22 Matthew 27.1–10	Psalms **72**, 76 *or* **148**, 149, 150 Hosea 8 1 Corinthians 12.1–11 *or, if the Presentation is celebrated on Sunday 31 January:* **1st EP of the Presentation:** Psalm 118; 1 Samuel 1.19*b*–end; Hebrews 4.11–end

If the Presentation of Christ in the Temple is celebrated on Tuesday 2 February:

			Principal Service	3rd Service	2nd Service
Sunday	**31 January** **4th Sunday of Epiphany**	*W*	Ezekiel 43.27—44.4 Psalm 48 1 Corinthians 13 Luke 2.22–40	Psalm 71.1–6, 15–17 Micah 6.1–8 1 Corinthians 6.12–end	Psalm 34 [34.1–10] 1 Chronicles 29.6–19 Acts 7.44–50 *HC* John 4.19–29*a*
			Holy Communion	**Morning Prayer**	**Evening Prayer**
Monday	**1 February** *Brigid, abbess, c.525* DEL week 4	*W*	2 Samuel 15.13–14, 30, 16.5–13 Psalm 3 Mark 5.1–20	Psalms **57**, 96 *or* **1**, 2, 3 Genesis 18.1–15 Matthew 27.11–26	**1st EP of the Presentation:** Psalm 118 1 Samuel 1.19*b*–end Hebrews 4.11–end
			Principal Service	**3rd Service**	**2nd Service**
Tuesday	**2 February** **Presentation of Christ in the Temple** (Candlemas)	*Gold or W*	Malachi 3.1–5 Psalm 24. [1–6] 7–end Hebrews 2.14–end Luke 2.22–40	*MP* Psalms **48**, 146 Exodus 13.1–16 Romans 12.1–5	*EP* Psalms 122, **132** Haggai 2.1–9 John 2.18–22

If the Presentation of Christ in the Temple is celebrated on Sunday 31 January:

			Principal Service	3rd Service	2nd Service
Sunday	**31 January** **Presentation of Christ in the Temple** (Candlemas)	*Gold or W*	Malachi 3.1–5 Psalm 24. [1–6] 7–end Hebrews 2.14–end Luke 2.22–40	*MP* Psalms **48**, 146 Exodus 13.1–16 Romans 12.1–5	*EP* Psalms 122, **132** Haggai 2.1–9 John 2.18–22
			Holy Communion	**Morning Prayer**	**Evening Prayer**
Monday	**1 February** *Brigid, abbess, c.525* Ordinary Time starts today if the Presentation was celebrated on 31 January DEL week 4	*G*	2 Samuel 15.13–14, 30, 16.5–13 Psalm 3 Mark 5.1–20	Psalms **1**, 2, 3 Genesis 18.1–15 Matthew 27.11–26	Psalms **4**, 7 Hosea 9 1 Corinthians 12.12–end
Tuesday	**2 February**	*G*	2 Samuel 18.9–10, 14, 24–25, 30—19.3 Psalm 86.1–6 Mark 5.21–end	Psalms **5**, 6 (8) Genesis 18.16–end Matthew 27.27–44	Psalms **9**, 10* Hosea 10 1 Corinthians 13

Epiphany 4

Wednesday	**3 February** *Gw* Anskar, archbishop, missionary, 865 (see p. 75) Ordinary Time starts today if the Presentation was celebrated on 2 February	2 Samuel 24.2, 9–17 Psalm 32.1–8 Mark 6.1–6*a*	Psalm **119.1–32** Genesis 19.1–3, 12–29 Matthew 27.45–56	Psalms **11**, 12, 13 Hosea 11.1–11 1 Corinthians 14.1–19
Thursday	**4 February** *G* *Gilbert, founder of the Gilbertine Order, 1189*	1 Kings 2.1–4, 10–12 *Canticle:* 1 Chronicles 29.10–12 *or* Psalm 145.1–5 Mark 6.7–13	Psalms 14, **15**, 16 Genesis 21.1–21 Matthew 27.57–end	Psalm **18*** Hosea 11.12—end of 12 1 Corinthians 14.20–end
Friday	**5 February** *G*	Ecclesiasticus 47.2–11 Psalm 18.31–36, 50–end Mark 6.14–29	Psalms 17, **19** Genesis 22.1–19 Matthew 28.1–15	Psalm **22** Hosea 13.1–14 1 Corinthians 16.1–9
Saturday	**6 February** *G* *Martyrs of Japan, 1597* *Accession of Queen Elizabeth II, 1952* (see p. 78)	1 Kings 3.4–13 Psalm 119.9–16 Mark 6.30–34	Psalms 20, 21, **23** Genesis 23 Matthew 28.16–end	Psalms **24**, 25 Hosea 14 1 Corinthians 16.10–end

			Principal Service	3rd Service	2nd Service
Sunday	**7 February** **2nd Sunday before Lent**	*G*	Genesis 2.4*b*–9, 15–end Psalm 65 Revelation 4 Luke 8.22–25	Psalm 104.1–26 Job 28.1–11 Acts 14.8–17	Psalm 147 [147.13–end] Genesis 1.1—2.3 Matthew 6.25–end
			Holy Communion	**Morning Prayer**	**Evening Prayer**
Monday	**8 February** DEL week 5	*G*	1 Kings 8.1–7, 9–13 Psalm 132.1–9 Mark 6.53–end	Psalms 27, **30** Genesis 29.31—30.24 2 Timothy 4.1–8	Psalms 26, **28**, 29 2 Chronicles 9.1–12 John 19.1–16
Tuesday	**9 February**	*G*	1 Kings 8.22–23, 27–30 Psalm 84.1–10 Mark 7.1–13	Psalms 32, **36** Genesis 31.1–24 2 Timothy 4.9–end	Psalm **33** 2 Chronicles 10.1—11.4 John 19.17–30
Wednesday	**10 February** *Scholastica, abbess, c.543*	*G*	1 Kings 10.1–10 Psalm 37.3–6, 30–32 Mark 7.14–23	Psalm **34** Genesis 31.25—32.2 Titus 1	Psalm **119.33–56** 2 Chronicles 12 John 19.31–end
Thursday	**11 February**	*G*	1 Kings 11.4–13 Psalm 106.3, 35–41 Mark 7.24–30	Psalm **37*** Genesis 32.3–30 Titus 2	Psalms 39, **40** 2 Chronicles 13.1—14.1 John 20.1–10
Friday	**12 February**	*G*	1 Kings 11.29–32, 12.19 Psalm 81.8–14 Mark 7.31–end	Psalm **31** Genesis 33.1–17 Titus 3	Psalm **35** 2 Chronicles 14.2–end John 20.11–18
Saturday	**13 February**	*G*	1 Kings 12.26–32, 13.33–end Psalm 106.6–7, 20–23 Mark 8.1–10	Psalms 41, **42**, 43 Genesis 35 Philemon	Psalms 45, **46** 2 Chronicles 15.1–15 John 20.19–end

Sunday next before Lent

			Principal Service	3rd Service	2nd Service
Sunday	**14 February** **Sunday next before Lent**	*G*	Exodus 34.29–end Psalm 99 2 Corinthians 3.12—4.2 Luke 9.28–36 [37–43*a*]	Psalm 2 Exodus 33.17–end 1 John 3.1–3	Psalm 89.1–18 [89.5–12] Exodus 3.1–6 John 12.27–36*a*
			Holy Communion	**Morning Prayer**	**Evening Prayer**
Monday	**15 February** *Sigfrid, bishop, 1045* *Thomas Bray, priest, founder of SPCK and SPG, 1730* DEL week 6	*G*	James 1.1–11 Psalm 119.65–72 Mark 8.11–13	Psalm **44** Genesis 37.1–11 Galatians 1	Psalms **47**, 49 Jeremiah 1 John 3.1–21
Tuesday	**16 February**	*G*	James 1.12–18 Psalm 94.12–18 Mark 8.14–21	Psalms **48**, 52 Genesis 37.12–end Galatians 2.1–10	Psalm **50** Jeremiah 2.1–13 John 3.22–end
			Principal Service	**3rd Service**	**2nd Service**
Wednesday	**17 February** **Ash Wednesday**	*P(La)*	Joel 2.1, 2, 12–17 *or* Isaiah 58.1–12 Psalm 51.1–18 2 Corinthians 5.20*b*—6.10 Matthew 6.1–6, 16–21 *or* John 8.1–11	*MP* Psalm **38** Daniel 9.3–6, 17–19 1 Timothy 6.6–19	*EP* Psalms **51** *or* 102 [102.1–18] Isaiah 1.10–18 Luke 15.11–end
			Holy Communion	**Morning Prayer**	**Evening Prayer**
Thursday	**18 February**	*P(La)*	Deuteronomy 30.15–end Psalm 1 Luke 9.22–25	Psalms **77** *or* 56, **57** (63*) Genesis 39 Galatians 2.11–end	Psalms **74** *or* 61, **62**, 64 Jeremiah 2.14–32 John 4.1–26
Friday	**19 February**	*P(La)*	Isaiah 58.1–9*a* Psalm 51.1–5, 17–18 Matthew 9.14–15	Psalms **3**, 7 *or* **51**, 54 Genesis 40 Galatians 3.1–14	Psalms **31** *or* **38** Jeremiah 3.6–22 John 4.27–42
Saturday	**20 February**	*P(La)*	Isaiah 58.9*b*–end Psalm 86.1–7 Luke 5.27–32	Psalms **71** *or* **68** Genesis 41.1–24 Galatians 3.15–22	Psalms **73** *or* 65, **66** Jeremiah 4.1–18 John 4.43–end

			Principal Service	3rd Service	2nd Service
Sunday	**21 February** **1st Sunday of Lent**	*P(La)*	Deuteronomy 26.1–11 Psalm 91.1, 2, 9–end [91.1–11] Romans 10.8*b*–13 Luke 4.1–13	Psalm 50.1–15 Micah 6.1–8 Luke 5.27–end	Psalm 119.73–88 Jonah 3 Luke 18.9–14
			Holy Communion	**Morning Prayer**	**Evening Prayer**
Monday	**22 February**	*P(La)*	Leviticus 19.1–2, 11–18 Psalm 19.7–end Matthew 25.31–end	Psalms 10, **11** *or* **71** Genesis 41.25–45 Galatians 3.23—4.7	Psalms 12, **13**, 14 *or* **72**, 75 Jeremiah 4.19–end John 5.1–18
Tuesday	**23 February** Polycarp, bishop, martyr, c.155 (see p. 72)	*P(La)r*	Isaiah 55.10–11 Psalm 34.4–6, 21–22 Matthew 6.7–15	Psalms **44** *or* **73** Genesis 41.46—42.5 Galatians 4.8–20	Psalms 46, **49** *or* **74** Jeremiah 5.1–19 John 5.19–29
Wednesday	**24 February** Ember Day	*P(La)*	Jonah 3 Psalm 51.1–5, 17–18 Luke 11.29–32	Psalms **6**, 17 *or* **77** Genesis 42.6–17 Galatians 4.21—5.1	Psalms 9, **28** *or* **119.81–104** Jeremiah 5.20–end John 5.30–end
Thursday	**25 February**	*P(La)*	Esther 14.1–5, 12–14 *or* Isaiah 55.6–9 Psalm 138 Matthew 7.7–12	Psalms **42**, 43 *or* **78.1–39*** Genesis 42.18–28 Galatians 5.2–15	Psalms 137, 138, **142** *or* **78.40–end*** Jeremiah 6.9–21 John 6.1–15
Friday	**26 February** Ember Day	*P(La)*	Ezekiel 18.21–28 Psalm 130 Matthew 5.20–26	Psalms **22** *or* **55** Genesis 42.29–end Galatians 5.16–end	Psalms 54, **55** *or* **69** Jeremiah 6.22–end John 6.16–27
Saturday	**27 February** George Herbert, priest, poet, 1633 (see p. 74) Ember Day	*P(La)w*	Deuteronomy 26.16–end Psalm 119.1–8 Matthew 5.43–end	Psalms 59, **63** *or* **76**, 79 Genesis 43.1–15 Galatians 6	Psalms **4**, 16 *or* 81, **84** Jeremiah 7.1–20 John 6.27–40

Lent 2

			Principal Service	3rd Service	2nd Service
Sunday	**28 February** **2nd Sunday of Lent**	*P(La)*	Genesis 15.1–12, 17–18 Psalm 27 Philippians 3.17—4.1 Luke 13.31–end	Psalm 119.161–end Genesis 17.1–7, 15–16 Romans 11.13–24	Psalm 135 [135.1–14] Jeremiah 22.1–9, 13–17 Luke 14.27–33
			Holy Communion	**Morning Prayer**	**Evening Prayer**
Monday	**1 March** David, bishop, patron of Wales, *c*.601 (see p. 74)	*P(La)w*	Daniel 9.4–10 Psalm 79.8–9, 12, 14 Luke 6.36–38	Psalms 26, **32** *or* **80**, 82 Genesis 43.16–end Hebrews 1	Psalms 70, **74** *or* **85**, 86 Jeremiah 7.21–end John 6.41–51
Tuesday	**2 March** Chad, bishop, missionary, 672 (see p. 75)	*P(La)w*	Isaiah 1.10, 16–20 Psalm 50.8, 16–end Matthew 23.1–12	Psalms **50** *or* 87, **89.1–18** Genesis 44.1–17 Hebrews 2.1–9	Psalms **52**, 53, 54 *or* **89.19–end** Jeremiah 8.1–15 John 6.52–59
Wednesday	**3 March**	*P(La)*	Jeremiah 18.18–20 Psalm 31.4–5, 14–18 Matthew 20.17–28	Psalm **35** *or* **119.105–128** Genesis 44.18–end Hebrews 2.10–end	Psalms **3**, 51 *or* **91**, 93 Jeremiah 8.18—9.11 John 6.60–end
Thursday	**4 March**	*P(La)*	Jeremiah 17.5–10 Psalm 1 Luke 16.19–end	Psalms **34** *or* 90, **92** Genesis 45.1–15 Hebrews 3.1–6	Psalms **71** *or* **94** Jeremiah 9.12–24 John 7.1–13
Friday	**5 March**	*P(La)*	Genesis 37.3–4, 12–13, 17–28 Psalm 105.16–22 Matthew 21.33–43, 45–46	Psalms 40, **41** *or* **88** (95) Genesis 45.16–end Hebrews 3.7–end	Psalms **6**, 38 *or* **102** Jeremiah 10.1–16 John 7.14–24
Saturday	**6 March**	*P(La)*	Micah 7.14–15, 18–20 Psalm 103.1–4, 9–12 Luke 15.1–3, 11–end	Psalms 3, **25** *or* 96, **97**, 100 Genesis 46.1–7, 28–end Hebrews 4.1–13	Psalms **23**, 27 *or* **104** Jeremiah 10.17–24 John 7.25–36

			Principal Service	3rd Service	2nd Service
Sunday	**7 March** **3rd Sunday of Lent**	*P(La)*	Isaiah 55.1–9 Psalm 63.1–9 1 Corinthians 10.1–13 Luke 13.1–9	Psalms 26, 28 Deuteronomy 6.4–9 John 17.1*a*, 11*b*–19	Psalms 12, 13 Genesis 28.10–19*a* John 1.35–end

			Holy Communion	Morning Prayer	Evening Prayer
	The following readings may replace those provided for Holy Communion on any day during the Third Week of Lent: Exodus 17.1–7; Psalm 95.1–2, 6–end; John 4.5–42				
Monday	**8 March** Edward King, bishop, 1910 (see p. 74) *Felix, bishop, 647* *Geoffrey Studdert Kennedy, priest, poet, 1929*	*P(La)w*	2 Kings 5.1–15 Psalms 42.1–2, 43.1–4 Luke 4.24–30	Psalms **5**, 7 *or* **98**, 99, 101 Genesis 47.1–27 Hebrews 4.14—5.10	Psalms 11, **17** *or* **105*** (*or* 103) Jeremiah 11.1–17 John 7.37–52
Tuesday	**9 March**	*P(La)*	Song of the Three 2, 11–20 *or* Daniel 2.20–23 Psalm 25.3–10 Matthew 18.21–end	Psalms 6, **9** *or* **106*** (*or* 103) Genesis 47.28—end of 48 Hebrews 5.11—6.12	Psalms 61, 62, **64** *or* **107*** Jeremiah 11.18—12.6 John 7.53—8.11
Wednesday	**10 March**	*P(La)*	Deuteronomy 4.1, 5–9 Psalm 147.13–end Matthew 5.17–19	Psalms **38** *or* 110, **111**, 112 Genesis 49.1–32 Hebrews 6.13–end	Psalms 36, **39** *or* **119.129–152** Jeremiah 13.1–11 John 8.12–30
Thursday	**11 March**	*P(La)*	Jeremiah 7.23–28 Psalm 95.1–2, 6–end Luke 11.14–23	Psalms **56**, 57 *or* 113, **115** Genesis 49.33—end of 50 Hebrews 7.1–10	Psalms **59**, 60 *or* 114, **116**, 117 Jeremiah 14 John 8.31–47
Friday	**12 March**	*P(La)*	Hosea 14 Psalm 81.6–10, 13, 16 Mark 12.28–34	Psalms **22** *or* **139** Exodus 1.1–14 Hebrews 7.11–end	Psalms **69** *or* **130**, 131, 137 Jeremiah 15.10–end John 8.48–end
Saturday	**13 March**	*P(La)*	Hosea 5.15—6.6 Psalm 51.1–2, 17–end Luke 18.9–14	Psalms **31** *or* 120, **121**, 122 Exodus 1.22—2.10 Hebrews 8	Psalms **116**, 130 *or* **118** Jeremiah 16.10—17.4 John 9.1–17

		Principal Service	3rd Service	2nd Service
Sunday	**14 March** *P(La)* **4th Sunday of Lent**	Joshua 5.9–12 Psalm 32 2 Corinthians 5.16–end Luke 15.1–3, 11*b*–end	Psalms 84, 85 Genesis 37.3–4, 12–end 1 Peter 2.16–end	Psalm 30 Prayer of Manasseh *or* Isaiah 40.27—41.13 2 Timothy 4.1–18 *HC* John 11.17–44

For Mothering Sunday:
Exodus 2.1–10 *or* 1 Samuel 1.20–end; Psalm 34.11–20 *or* 127.1–4;
2 Corinthians 1.3–7 *or* Colossians 3.12–17; Luke 2.33–35 *or* John 19.25*b*–27
If the Principal Service readings have been displaced by Mothering Sunday provisions, they may be used at the Second Service.

		Holy Communion	Morning Prayer	Evening Prayer

The following readings may replace those provided for Holy Communion on any day (except St Joseph's Day) during the Fourth Week of Lent: Micah 7.7–9; Psalm 27.1, 9–10, 16–17; John 9

		Holy Communion	Morning Prayer	Evening Prayer
Monday	**15 March** *P(La)*	Isaiah 65.17–21 Psalm 30.1–5, 8, 11–end John 4.43–end	Psalms 70, **77** *or* 123, 124, 125, **126** Exodus 2.11–22 Hebrews 9.1–14	Psalms **25**, 28 *or* **127**, 128, 129 Jeremiah 17.5–18 John 9.18–end
Tuesday	**16 March** *P(La)*	Ezekiel 47.1–9, 12 Psalm 46.1–8 John 5.1–3, 5–16	Psalms 54, **79** *or* **132**, 133 Exodus 2.23—3.20 Hebrews 9.15–end	Psalms **80**, 82 *or* (134,) **135** Jeremiah 18.1–12 John 10.1–10
Wednesday	**17 March** *P(La)w* Patrick, bishop, missionary, patron of Ireland, *c.*460 (see p. 75)	Isaiah 49.8–15 Psalm 145.8–18 John 5.17–30	Psalms 63, **90** *or* **119.153–end** Exodus 4.1–23 Hebrews 10.1–18	Psalms 52, **91** *or* **136** Jeremiah 18.13–end John 10.11–21
Thursday	**18 March** *P(La)* *Cyril, bishop, teacher of the faith, 386*	Exodus 32.7–14 Psalm 106.19–23 John 5.31–end	Psalms 53, **86** *or* **143**, 146 Exodus 4.27—6.1 Hebrews 10.19–25	Psalms **94** *or* **138**, 140, 141 Jeremiah 19.1–13 John 10.22–end *or:* 1st EP of Joseph of Nazareth: Psalm 132; Hosea 11.1–9; Luke 2.41–end

		Principal Service	3rd Service	2nd Service
Friday	**19 March** *W* Joseph of Nazareth	2 Samuel 7.4–16 Psalm 89.26–36 Romans 4.13–18 Matthew 1.18–end	*MP* Psalms 25, 147.1–12 Isaiah 11.1–10 Matthew 13.54–end	*EP* Psalms 1, 112 Genesis 50.22–end Matthew 2.13–end

		Holy Communion	Morning Prayer	Evening Prayer
Saturday	**20 March** *P(La)w* Cuthbert, bishop, missionary, 687 (see p. 75)	Jeremiah 11.18–20 Psalm 7.1–2, 8–10 John 7.40–52	Psalms **32** *or* **147** Exodus 7.8–end Hebrews 11.1–16	Psalms **140**, 141, 142 *or* **148**, 149, 150 Jeremiah 20.7–end John 11.17–27

			Principal Service	3rd Service	2nd Service
Sunday	**21 March** **5th Sunday of Lent** *Passiontide begins*	*P(La)*	Isaiah 43.16–21 Psalm 126 Philippians 3.4*b*–14 John 12.1–8	Psalms 111, 112 Isaiah 35 Romans 7.21—8.4	Psalm 35 [35.1–9] 2 Chronicles 35.1–6, 10–16 Luke 22.1–13

			Holy Communion	Morning Prayer	Evening Prayer
	The following readings may replace those provided for Holy Communion on any day (except the Annunciation of Our Lord) during the Fifth Week of Lent: 2 Kings 4.18–21, 32–37; Psalm 17.1–8, 16; John 11.1–45				
Monday	**22 March**	*P(La)*	Susannah 1–9, 15–17, 19–30, 33–62 [41*b*–62] *or* Joshua 2.1–14 Psalm 23 John 8.1–11	Psalms **73**, 121 *or* **1**, 2, 3 Exodus 8.1–19 Hebrews 11.17–31	Psalms **26**, 27 *or* **4**, 7 Jeremiah 21.1–10 John 11.28–44
Tuesday	**23 March**	*P(La)*	Numbers 21.4–9 Psalm 102.1–3, 16–23 John 8.21–30	Psalms **35**, 123 *or* **5**, 6 (8) Exodus 8.20–end Hebrews 11.32—12.2	Psalms **61**, 64 *or* **9**, 10* Jeremiah 22.1–5, 13–19 John 11.45–end
Wednesday	**24 March** *Walter Hilton, mystic, 1396* *Oscar Romero, archbishop, martyr, 1980*	*P(La)*	Daniel 3.14–20, 24–25, 28 *Canticle:* Bless the Lord John 8.31–42	Psalms **55**, 124 *or* **119.1–32** Exodus 9.1–12 Hebrews 12.3–13	1st EP of the **Annunciation of Our Lord to the BVM:** Psalm 85 Wisdom 9.1–12 *or* Genesis 3.8–15 Galatians 4.1–5

			Principal Service	3rd Service	2nd Service
Thursday	**25 March** **Annunciation of Our Lord to the Blessed Virgin Mary**	*Gold or W*	Isaiah 7.10–14 Psalm 40.5–11 Hebrews 10.4–10 Luke 1.26–38	*MP* Psalms 111, 113 1 Samuel 2.1–10 Romans 5.12–end	*EP* Psalms 131, 146 Isaiah 52.1–12 Hebrews 2.5–end

			Holy Communion	Morning Prayer	Evening Prayer
Friday	**26 March** *Harriet Monsell, founder of the Community of St John the Baptist, 1883*	*P(La)*	Jeremiah 20.10–13 Psalm 18.1–6 John 10.31–end	Psalms **22**, 126 *or* 17, **19** Exodus 10 Hebrews 13.1–16	Psalms **31** *or* **22** Jeremiah 24 John 12.20–36*a*
Saturday	**27 March**	*P(La)*	Ezekiel 37.21–end *Canticle:* Jeremiah 31.10–13 *or* Psalm 121 John 11.45–end	Psalms **23**, 127 *or* 20, 21, **23** Exodus 11 Hebrews 13.17–end	Psalms 128, 129, **130** *or* **24**, 25 Jeremiah 25.1–14 John 12.36*b*–end

Holy Week

			Principal Service		3rd Service	2nd Service
Sunday	**28 March** **Palm Sunday**	*R*	*Liturgy of the Palms:* Luke 19.28–40 Psalm 118.1–2, 19–end [118.19–24]	*Liturgy of the Passion:* Isaiah 50.4–9*a* Psalm 31.9–16 [31.9–18] Philippians 2.5–11 Luke 22.14–end of 23 *or* Luke 23.1–49	Psalms 61, 62 Zechariah 9.9–12 1 Corinthians 2.1–12	Psalm 69.1–20 Isaiah 5.1–7 Luke 20.9–19
			Holy Communion		**Morning**	**Evening**
					From the Monday of Holy Week until the Saturday of Easter Week the seasonal psalmody must be used.	
Monday	**29 March** Monday of Holy Week	*R*	Isaiah 42.1–9 Psalm 36.5–11 Hebrews 9.11–15 John 12.1–11		Psalm 41 Lamentations 1.1–12*a* Luke 22.1–23	Psalm 25 Lamentations 2.8–19 Colossians 1.18–23
Tuesday	**30 March** Tuesday of Holy Week	*R*	Isaiah 49.1–7 Psalm 71.1–8 [9–14] 1 Corinthians 1.18–31 John 12.20–36		Psalm 27 Lamentations 3.1–18 Luke 22. [24–38] 39–53	Psalm 55.13–24 Lamentations 3.40–51 Galatians 6.11–end
Wednesday	**31 March** Wednesday of Holy Week	*R*	Isaiah 50.4–9*a* Psalm 70 Hebrews 12.1–3 John 13.21–32		Psalm 102 [102.1–18] Wisdom 1.16—2.1, 12–22 *or* Jeremiah 11.18–20 Luke 22.54–end	Psalm 88 Isaiah 63.1–9 Revelation 14.18—15.4
Thursday	**1 April** **Maundy Thursday**	*W*	Exodus 12.1–4 [5–10], 11–14 Psalm 116.1, 10–end [116.9–end] 1 Corinthians 11.23–26 John 13.1–17, 31*b*–35		Psalms 42, 43 Leviticus 16.2–24 Luke 23.1–25	Psalm 39 Exodus 11 Ephesians 2.11–18
Friday	**2 April** **Good Friday**	*Hangings removed; R for the Liturgy*	Isaiah 52.13—end of 53 Psalm 22 *or* 22.1–11 [1–21] Hebrews 10.16–25 *or* 4.14–16; 5.7–9 John 18.1–end of 19		Psalm 69 Genesis 22.1–18 A part of John 18 and 19 may be read, if not used at the Principal Service *or* Hebrews 10.1–10	Psalms 130, 143 Lamentations 5.15–end John 19.38–end *or* Colossians 1.18–23

		Holy Communion	Morning Prayer	Evening Prayer
Saturday	**3 April** *Hangings removed* **Easter Eve** *These readings are for use at services other than the Easter Vigil.*	Job 14.1–14 *or* Lamentations 3.1–9, 19–24 Psalm 31.1–4, 15–16 [31.1–5] 1 Peter 4.1–8 Matthew 27.57–end *or* John 19.38–end	Psalm 142 Hosea 6.1–6 John 2.18–22	Psalm 116 Job 19.21–27 1 John 5.5–12

		Vigil Readings	Complementary Psalmody
Saturday *or* **Sunday**	**3 April evening** *Gold or W* **4 April morning** *Easter Vigil* *The New Testament readings should be preceded by a minimum of three Old Testament readings.* *The Exodus reading should always be used.*	Genesis 1.1–2.4*a* Genesis 7.1–5, 11–18; 8.6–18; 9.8–13 Genesis 22.1–18 **Exodus 14.10–end; 15.20–21** Isaiah 55.1–11 Baruch 3.9–15, 32—4.4 *or* Proverbs 8.1–8, 19–21; 9.4*b*–6 Ezekiel 36.24–28 Ezekiel 37.1–14 Zephaniah 3.14–end **Romans 6.3–11** **Luke 24.1–12**	Psalm 136.1–9, 23–end Psalm 46 Psalm 16 *Canticle:* **Exodus 15.1*b*–13, 17–18** *Canticle:* Isaiah 12.2–end Psalm 19 Psalms 42, 43 Psalm 143 Psalm 98 **Psalm 114**

		Principal Service	3rd Service	2nd Service
Sunday	**4 April** *Gold or W* **Easter Day**	Acts 10.34–43† *or* Isaiah 65.17–end Psalm 118.[1–2] 14–24 1 Corinthians 15.19–26 *or* Acts 10.34–43† John 20.1–18 *or* Luke 24.1–12 † *The reading from Acts must be used as either the first or second reading.*	*MP* Psalms 114, 117 Ezekiel 47.1–12 John 2.13–22	*EP* Psalm 105 *or* 66.1–11 Isaiah 43.1–21 1 Corinthians 15.1–11 *or* John 20.19–23

Easter Week

			Holy Communion	Morning Prayer	Evening Prayer
Monday	**5 April** Monday in Easter Week	W	Acts 2.14, 22–32 Psalm 16.1–2, 6–end Matthew 28.8–15	Psalms **111**, 117, 146 Exodus 12.1–14 1 Corinthians 15.1–11	Psalm **135** Song of Solomon 1.9—2.7 Mark 16.1–8
Tuesday	**6 April** Tuesday in Easter Week	W	Acts 2.36–41 Psalm 33.4–5, 18–end John 20.11–18	Psalms **112**, 147.1–12 Exodus 12.14–36 1 Corinthians 15.12–19	Psalm **136** Song of Solomon 2.8–end Luke 24.1–12
Wednesday	**7 April** Wednesday in Easter Week	W	Acts 3.1–10 Psalm 105.1–9 Luke 24.13–35	Psalms **113**, 147.13–end Exodus 12.37–end 1 Corinthians 15.20–28	Psalm **105** Song of Solomon 3 Matthew 28.16–end
Thursday	**8 April** Thursday in Easter Week	W	Acts 3.11–26 Psalm 8 Luke 24.35–48	Psalms **114**, 148 Exodus 13.1–16 1 Corinthians 15.29–34	Psalm **106** Song of Solomon 5.2—6.3 Luke 7.11–17
Friday	**9 April** Friday in Easter Week	W	Acts 4.1–12 Psalm 118.1–4, 22–26 John 21.1–14	Psalms **115**, 149 Exodus 13.17—14.14 1 Corinthians 15.35–50	Psalm **107** Song of Solomon 7.10—8.4 Luke 8.41–end
Saturday	**10 April** Saturday in Easter Week	W	Acts 4.13–21 Psalm 118.1–4, 14–21 Mark 16.9–15	Psalms **116**, 150 Exodus 14.15–end 1 Corinthians 15.51–end	Psalm **145** Song of Solomon 8.5–7 John 11.17–44

			Principal Service	3rd Service	2nd Service
Sunday	**11 April** **2nd Sunday of Easter**	W	[Exodus 14.10–end; 15.20–21] Acts 5.27–32† Psalm 118.14–end *or* Psalm 150 Revelation 1.4–8 John 20.19–end	Psalm 136.1–16 Exodus 12.1–13 1 Peter 1.3–12	Psalm 16 Isaiah 52.13—53.12 *or* 53.1–6, 9–12 Luke 24.13–35

† *The reading from Acts must be used as either the first or second reading.*

			Holy Communion	Morning Prayer	Evening Prayer
Monday	**12 April**	W	Acts 4.23–31 Psalm 2.1–9 John 3.1–8	Psalms 2, **19** *or* **1**, 2, 3 Exodus 15.1–21 Colossians 1.1–14	Psalms **139** *or* **4**, 7 Deuteronomy 1.3–18 John 20.1–10
Tuesday	**13 April**	W	Acts 4.32–end Psalm 93 John 3.7–15	Psalms **8**, 20, 21 *or* **5**, 6 (8) Exodus 15.22—16.10 Colossians 1.15–end	Psalms **104** *or* **9**, 10* Deuteronomy 1.19–40 John 20.11–18
Wednesday	**14 April**	W	Acts 5.17–26 Psalm 34.1–8 John 3.16–21	Psalms 16, **30** *or* **119.1–32** Exodus 16.11–end Colossians 2.1–15	Psalms **33** *or* **11**, 12, 13 Deuteronomy 3.18–end John 20.19–end
Thursday	**15 April**	W	Acts 5.27–33 Psalm 34.1, 15–end John 3.31–end	Psalms **28**, 29 *or* 14, **15**, 16 Exodus 17 Colossians 2.16—3.11	Psalm **34** *or* **18*** Deuteronomy 4.1–14 John 21.1–14
Friday	**16 April** *Isabella Gilmore, deaconess, 1923*	W	Acts 5.34–42 Psalm 27.1–5, 16–17 John 6.1–15	Psalms 57, **61** *or* 17, **19** Exodus 18.1–12 Colossians 3.12—4.1	Psalms **118** *or* **22** Deuteronomy 4.15–31 John 21.15–19
Saturday	**17 April**	W	Acts 6.1–7 Psalm 33.1–5, 18–19 John 6.16–21	Psalms 63, **84** *or* 20, 21, **23** Exodus 18.13–end Colossians 4.2–end	Psalms **66** *or* **24**, 25 Deuteronomy 4.32–40 John 21.20–end

Easter 3

			Principal Service	3rd Service	2nd Service
Sunday	**18 April** **3rd Sunday of Easter**	*W*	[Zephaniah 3.14–end] Acts 9.1–6 [7–20] † Psalm 30 Revelation 5.11–end John 21.1–19	Psalm 80.1–8 Exodus 15.1–2, 9–18 John 10.1–19	Psalm 86 Isaiah 38.9–20 John 11.[17–26] 27–44

† *The reading from Acts must be used as either the first or second reading.*

			Holy Communion	Morning Prayer	Evening Prayer
Monday	**19 April** Alphege, archbishop, martyr, 1012 (see p. 72)	*Wr*	Acts 6.8–15 Psalm 119.17–24 John 6.22–29	Psalms **96**, 97 *or* 27, **30** Exodus 19 Luke 1.1–25	Psalms **61**, 65 *or* 26, **28**, 29 Deuteronomy 5.1–22 Ephesians 1.1–14
Tuesday	**20 April**	*W*	Acts 7.51—8.1*a* Psalm 31.1–5, 16 John 6.30–35	Psalms **98**, 99, 100 *or* 32, **36** Exodus 20.1–21 Luke 1.26–38	Psalm **71** *or* **33** Deuteronomy 5.22–end Ephesians 1.15–end
Wednesday	**21 April** Anselm, abbot, archbishop, teacher of the faith, 1109 (see p. 73)	*W*	Acts 8.1*b*–8 Psalm 66.1–6 John 6.35–40	Psalm **105** *or* **34** Exodus 24 Luke 1.39–56	Psalms 67, **72** *or* **119.33–56** Deuteronomy 6 Ephesians 2.1–10
Thursday	**22 April**	*W*	Acts 8.26–end Psalm 66.7–8, 14–end John 6.44–51	Psalm **136** *or* **37*** Exodus 25.1–22 Luke 1.57–end	Psalms **73** *or* 39, **40** Deuteronomy 7.1–11 Ephesians 2.11–end *or:* 1st EP of George, martyr, patron of England: Psalms 111, 116; Jeremiah 15.15–end; Hebrews 11.32—12.2

			Principal Service	3rd Service	2nd Service
Friday	**23 April** George, martyr, patron of England, *c*.304	*R*	1 Maccabees 2.59–64 *or* Revelation 12.7–12 Psalm 126 2 Timothy 2.3–13 John 15.18–21	*MP* Psalms 5, 146 Joshua 1.1–9 Ephesians 6.10–20	*EP* Psalms 3, 11 Isaiah 43.1–7 John 15.1–8

			Holy Communion	Morning Prayer	Evening Prayer
Saturday	**24 April** *Mellitus, bishop, 624*	*W*	Acts 9.31–42 Psalm 116.10–15 John 6.60–69	Psalms 108, **110**, 111 *or* 41, **42**, 43 Exodus 29.1–9 Luke 2.21–40	Psalms 23, **27** *or* 45, **46** Deuteronomy 8 Ephesians 3.14–end

			Principal Service	3rd Service	2nd Service
Sunday	**25 April** **4th Sunday of Easter**	*W*	[Genesis 7.1–5, 11–18; 8.6–18; 9.8–13] Acts 9.36–end† Psalm 23 Revelation 7.9–end John 10.22–30 † *The reading from Acts must be used as either the first or second reading.*	Psalm 146 1 Kings 17.17–end Luke 7.11–23	Psalms 113, 114 Isaiah 63.7–14 Luke 24.36–49 *or:* 1st EP of Mark the Evangelist: Psalm 19; Isaiah 52.7–10; Mark 1.1–15
Monday	**26 April** Mark the Evangelist *(transferred from 25 April)*	*R*	Proverbs 15.28–end *or* Acts 15.35–end Psalm 119.9–16 Ephesians 4.7–16 Mark 13.5–13	*MP* Psalms 37.23–end, 148 Isaiah 62.6–10 *or* Ecclesiasticus 51.13–end Acts 12.25—13.13	*EP* Psalm 45 Ezekiel 1.4–14 2 Timothy 4.1–11

			Holy Communion	Morning Prayer	Evening Prayer
Tuesday	**27 April** *Christina Rossetti, poet, 1894*	*W*	Acts 11.19–26 Psalm 87 John 10.22–30	Psalms **139** *or* **48**, 52 Exodus 32.15–34 Luke 3.1–14	Psalms 115, **116** *or* **50** Deuteronomy 9.23—10.5 Ephesians 4.17–end
Wednesday	**28 April** *Peter Chanel, missionary, martyr, 1841*	*W*	Acts 12.24—13.5 Psalm 67 John 12.44–end	Psalm **135** *or* **119.57–80** Exodus 33 Luke 3.15–22	Psalms **47**, 48 *or* **59**, 60 (67) Deuteronomy 10.12–end Ephesians 5.1–14
Thursday	**29 April** Catherine of Siena, teacher of the faith, 1380 (see p. 73)	*W*	Acts 13.13–25 Psalm 89.1–2, 20–26 John 13.16–20	Psalms **118** *or* 56, **57** (63*) Exodus 34.1–10, 27–end Luke 4.1–13	Psalms 81, **85** *or* 61, **62**, 64 Deuteronomy 11.8–end Ephesians 5.15–end
Friday	**30 April** *Pandita Mary Ramabai, translator, 1922*	*W*	Acts 13.26–33 Psalm 2 John 14.1–6	Psalms **33** *or* **51**, 54 Exodus 35.20—36.7 Luke 4.14–30	Psalms **36**, 40 *or* **38** Deuteronomy 12.1–14 Ephesians 6.1–9 *or:* 1st EP of Philip and James, Apostles: Psalm 25; Isaiah 40.27–end; John 12.20–26

			Principal Service	3rd Service	2nd Service
Saturday	**1 May** Philip and James, Apostles	*R*	Isaiah 30.15–21 Psalm 119.1–8 Ephesians 1.3–10 John 14.1–14	*MP* Psalms 139, 146 Proverbs 4.10–18 James 1.1–12	*EP* Psalm 149 Job 23.1–12 John 1.43–end

Easter 5

			Principal Service	3rd Service	2nd Service
Sunday	**2 May** **5th Sunday of Easter**	W	[Baruch 3.9–15, 32—4.4 *or* Genesis 22.1–18] Acts 11.1–18† Psalm 148 [148.1–6] Revelation 21.1–6 John 13.31–35	Psalm 16 2 Samuel 7.4–13 Acts 2.14*a*, 22–32 [33–36]	Psalm 98 Daniel 6.[1–5] 6–23 Mark 15.46—16.8

† *The reading from Acts must be used as either the first or second reading.*

			Holy Communion	Morning Prayer	Evening Prayer
Monday	**3 May**	W	Acts 14.5–18 Psalm 118.1–3, 14–15 John 14.21–26	Psalms **145** *or* **71** Numbers 9.15–end, 10.33–end Luke 4.38–end	Psalms **105** *or* **72**, 75 Deuteronomy 16.1–20 1 Peter 1.1–12
Tuesday	**4 May** English saints and martyrs of the Reformation era	W	Acts 14.19–end Psalm 145.10–end John 14.27–end *Lesser Festival eucharistic lectionary:* Isaiah 43.1–7 *or* Ecclesiasticus 2.10–17; Psalm 87; 2 Corinthians 4.5–12; John 12.20–26	Psalms **19**, 147.1–12 *or* **73** Numbers 11.1–33 Luke 5.1–11	Psalms 96, **97** *or* **74** Deuteronomy 17.8–end 1 Peter 1.13–end
Wednesday	**5 May**	W	Acts 15.1–6 Psalm 122.1–5 John 15.1–8	Psalms **30**, 147.13–end *or* **77** Numbers 12 Luke 5.12–26	Psalms 98, **99**, 100 *or* **119.81–104** Deuteronomy 18.9–end 1 Peter 2.1–10
Thursday	**6 May**	W	Acts 15.7–21 Psalm 96.1–3, 7–10 John 15.9–11	Psalms **57**, 148 *or* **78.1–39*** Numbers 13.1–3, 17–end Luke 5.27–end	Psalm **104** *or* **78.40–end*** Deuteronomy 19 1 Peter 2.11–end
Friday	**7 May**	W	Acts 15.22–31 Psalm 57.8–end John 15.12–17	Psalms **138**, 149 *or* **55** Numbers 14.1–25 Luke 6.1–11	Psalms **66** *or* **69** Deuteronomy 21.22—22.8 1 Peter 3.1–12
Saturday	**8 May** Julian of Norwich, spiritual writer, c.1417 (see p. 75)	W	Acts 16.1–10 Psalm 100 John 15.18–21	Psalms **146**, 150 *or* **76**, 79 Numbers 14.26–end Luke 6.12–26	Psalms **118** *or* 81, **84** Deuteronomy 24.5–end 1 Peter 3.13–end

Day	Date	Colour	Principal Service	3rd Service	2nd Service
Sunday	**9 May** **6th Sunday of Easter**	W	[Ezekiel 37.1–14] Acts 16.9–15† Psalm 67 Revelation 21.10, 22—22.5 John 14.23–29 *or* John 5.1–9 † *The reading from Acts must be used as either the first or second reading.*	Psalm 40.1–9 Genesis 1.26–28 [29–end] Colossians 3.1–11	Psalms 126, 127 Zephaniah 3.14–end Matthew 28.1–10, 16–end
			Holy Communion	**Morning Prayer**	**Evening Prayer**
Monday	**10 May** *Rogation Day*	W	Acts 16.11–15 Psalm 149.1–5 John 15.26—16.4	Psalms **65**, 67 *or* **80**, 82 Numbers 16.1–35 Luke 6.27–38	Psalms **121**, 122, 123 *or* **85**, 86 Deuteronomy 26 1 Peter 4.1–11
Tuesday	**11 May** *Rogation Day*	W	Acts 16.22–34 Psalm 138 John 16.5–11	Psalms 124, 125, **126**, 127 *or* 87, **89.1–18** Numbers 16.36–end Luke 6.39–end	Psalms **128**, 129, 130, 131 *or* **89.19–end** Deuteronomy 28.1–14 1 Peter 4.12–end
Wednesday	**12 May** *Rogation Day*	W	Acts 17.15, 22—18.1 Psalm 148.1–2, 11–end John 16.12–15	Psalms **132**, 133 *or* **119.105–128** Numbers 17.1–11 Luke 7.1–10	**1st EP of Ascension Day:** Psalms 15, 24 2 Samuel 23.1–5 Colossians 2.20—3.4
			Principal Service	**3rd Service**	**2nd Service**
Thursday	**13 May** **Ascension Day**	*Gold or W*	Acts 1.1–11† *or* Daniel 7.9–14 Psalm 47 *or* 93 Ephesians 1.15–end *or* Acts 1.1–11† Luke 24.44–end † *The reading from Acts must be used as either the first or second reading.*	*MP* Psalms 110, 150 Isaiah 52.7–end Hebrews 7.[11–25] 26–end	*EP* Psalm 8 Song of the Three vv 29–37 *or* 2 Kings 2.1–15 Revelation 5 *HC* Matthew 28.16–end
Friday	**14 May** Matthias the Apostle	*R*	Isaiah 22.15–end *or* Acts 1.15–end Psalm 15 Acts 1.15–end *or* 1 Corinthians 4.1–7 John 15.9–17	*MP* Psalms 16, 147.1–12 1 Samuel 2.27–35 Acts 2.37–end	*EP* Psalm 80 1 Samuel 16.1–13*a* Matthew 7.15–27
			Holy Communion	**Morning Prayer**	**Evening Prayer**
				From 15 to 22 May, in preparation for the Day of Pentecost, an alternative sequence of daily readings for use at one of the offices is marked with an asterisk.*	
Saturday	**15 May**	W	Acts 18.22–end Psalm 47.1–2, 7–end John 16.23–28	Psalms 21, **47** *or* 96, **97**, 100 Numbers 21.4–9 Luke 7.18–35 **Numbers 11.16–17, 24–29; 1 Corinthians 2*	Psalms 84, **85** *or* **104** Deuteronomy 30 1 John 2.7–17

Easter 7

			Principal Service	3rd Service	2nd Service
Sunday	**16 May** **7th Sunday of Easter** *Sunday after Ascension Day*	*W*	[Ezekiel 36.24–28] Acts 16.16–34† Psalm 97 Revelation 22.12–14, 16–17, 20–end John 17.20–end	Psalm 99 Deuteronomy 34 Luke 24.44–end *or* Acts 1.1–8	Psalm 68 [68.1–13, 18–19] Isaiah 44.1–8 Ephesians 4.7–16 *HC* Luke 24.44–end

† *The reading from Acts must be used as either the first or second reading.*

			Holy Communion	Morning Prayer	Evening Prayer
Monday	**17 May**	*W*	Acts 19.1–8 Psalm 68.1–6 John 16.29–end	Psalms **93**, 96, 97 *or* **98**, 99, 101 Numbers 22.1–35 Luke 7.36–end **Numbers 27.15–end; 1 Corinthians 3*	Psalms **18** *or* **105*** (*or* 103) Deuteronomy 31.1–13 1 John 2.18–end
Tuesday	**18 May**	*W*	Acts 20.17–27 Psalm 68.9–10, 18–19 John 17.1–11	Psalms 98, **99**, 100 *or* **106*** (*or* 103) Numbers 22.36—23.12 Luke 8.1–15 **1 Samuel 10.1–10; 1 Corinthians 12.1–13*	Psalms **68** *or* **107*** Deuteronomy 31.14–29 1 John 3.1–10
Wednesday	**19 May** Dunstan, archbishop, monastic reformer, 988 (see p. 74)	*W*	Acts 20.28–end Psalm 68.27–28, 32–end John 17.11–19	Psalms 2, **29** *or* 110, **111**, 112 Numbers 23.13–end Luke 8.16–25 **1 Kings 19.1–18; Matthew 3.13–end*	Psalms 36, **46** *or* **119.129–152** Deuteronomy 31.30—32.14 1 John 3.11–end
Thursday	**20 May** Alcuin, deacon, abbot, 804 (see p. 75)	*W*	Acts 22.30, 23.6–11 Psalm 16.1, 5–end John 17.20–end	Psalms **24**, 72 *or* 113, **115** Numbers 24 Luke 8.26–39 **Ezekiel 11.14–20; Matthew 9.35—10.20*	Psalms **139** *or* 114, **116**, 117 Deuteronomy 32.15–47 1 John 4.1–6
Friday	**21 May** *Helena, protector of the Holy Places, 330*	*W*	Acts 25.13–21 Psalm 103.1–2, 11–12, 19–20 John 21.15–19	Psalms **28**, 30 *or* **139** Numbers 27.12–end Luke 8.40–end **Ezekiel 36.22–28; Matthew 12.22–32*	Psalms **147** *or* **130**, 131, 137 Deuteronomy 33 1 John 4.7–end
Saturday	**22 May**	*W*	Acts 28.16–20, 30–end Psalm 11.4–end John 21.20–end	Psalms 42, **43** *or* 120, **121**, 122 Numbers 32.1–27 Luke 9.1–17 **Micah 3.1–8; Ephesians 6.10–20*	**1st EP of Pentecost:** Psalm **48** Deuteronomy 16.9–15 John 7.37–39

		Principal Service	3rd Service	2nd Service
Sunday	**23 May** *R* **Pentecost** *Whit Sunday*	Acts 2.1–21† *or* Genesis 11.1–9 Psalm 104.26–36, 37*b* [104.26–end] Romans 8.14–17 *or* Acts 2.1–21† John 14.8–17 [25–27]	*MP* Psalms 36.5–10; 150 Isaiah 40.12–23 *or* Wisdom 9.9–17 1 Corinthians 2.6–end	*EP* Psalm 33.1–12 Exodus 33.7–20 2 Corinthians 3.4–end *HC* John 16.4*b*–15

† *The reading from Acts must be used as either the first or second reading.*

		Holy Communion	Morning Prayer	Evening Prayer
Monday	**24 May** *Gw* John and Charles Wesley, evangelists, hymn writers, 1791 and 1788 (see p. 74) Ordinary Time resumes DEL week 8	1 Peter 1.3–9 Psalm 111 Mark 10.17–27	Psalms 123, 124, 125, **126** Joshua 1 Luke 9.18–27	Psalms **127**, 128, 129 2 Chronicles 17.1–12 Romans 1.1–17
Tuesday	**25 May** *Gw* The Venerable Bede, monk, scholar, historian, 735 (see p. 75) *Aldhelm, bishop, 709*	1 Peter 1.10–16 Psalm 98.1–5 Mark 10.28–31	Psalms **132**, 133 Joshua 2 Luke 9.28–36	Psalms (134), **135** 2 Chronicles 18.1–27 Romans 1.18–end
Wednesday	**26 May** *Gw* Augustine, archbishop, 605 (see p. 74) *John Calvin, reformer, 1564* *Philip Neri, founder of the Oratorians, spiritual guide, 1595*	1 Peter 1.18–end Psalm 147.13–end Mark 10.32–45	Psalm **119.153–end** Joshua 3 Luke 9.37–50	Psalm **136** 2 Chronicles 18.28—end of 19 Romans 2.1–16
Thursday	**27 May** *G*	1 Peter 2.2–5, 9–12 Psalm 100 Mark 10.46–end	Psalms **143**, 146 Joshua 4.1—5.1 Luke 9.51–end	Psalms **138**, 140, 141 2 Chronicles 20.1–23 Romans 2.17–end
Friday	**28 May** *G* *Lanfranc, monk, archbishop, scholar, 1089*	1 Peter 4.7–13 Psalm 96.10–end Mark 11.11–26	Psalms 142, **144** Joshua 5.2–end Luke 10.1–16	Psalm **145** 2 Chronicles 22.10—end of 23 Romans 3.1–20
Saturday	**29 May** *G*	Jude 17, 20–end Psalm 63.1–6 Mark 11.27–end	Psalm **147** Joshua 6.1–20 Luke 10.17–24	**1st EP of Trinity Sunday:** Psalms 97, 98 Isaiah 40.12–end Mark 1.1–13

Trinity Sunday

			Principal Service	3rd Service	2nd Service
Sunday	**30 May** **Trinity Sunday**	*Gold or W*	Proverbs 8.1–4, 22–31 Psalm 8 Romans 5.1–5 John 16.12–15	*MP* Psalm 29 Isaiah 6.1–8 Revelation 4	*EP* Psalm 73.1–3, 16–end Exodus 3.1–15 John 3.1–17
Monday	**31 May** Visit of the Blessed Virgin Mary to Elizabeth	*W*	Zephaniah 3.14–18 Psalm 113 Romans 12.9–16 Luke 1.39–49 [50–56]	*MP* Psalms 85, 150 1 Samuel 2.1–10 Mark 3.31–end	*EP* Psalms 122, 127, 128 Zechariah 2.10–end John 3.25–30

			Holy Communion	Morning Prayer	Evening Prayer
Tuesday	**1 June** Justin, martyr, *c.*165 (see p. 72) DEL week 9	*Gr*	2 Peter 3.11–15*a*, 17–end Psalm 90.1–4, 10, 14, 16 Mark 12.13–17	Psalms **5**, 6 (8) Joshua 7.16–end Luke 10.38–end	Psalms **9**, 10* 2 Chronicles 28 Romans 4.13–end
Wednesday	**2 June**	*G*	2 Timothy 1.1–3, 6–12 Psalm 123 Mark 12.18–27	Psalm **119.1–32** Joshua 8.1–29 Luke 11.1–13	Psalms **11**, 12, 13 2 Chronicles 29.1–19 Romans 5.1–11 *or:* 1st EP of Corpus Christi: Psalms 110, 111; Exodus 16.2–15; John 6.22–35

			Principal Service	3rd Service	2nd Service
Thursday	**3 June** Day of Thanksgiving for the Institution of the Holy Communion (Corpus Christi)	*W*	Genesis 14.18–20 Psalm 116.10–end 1 Corinthians 11.23–26 John 6.51–58	*MP* Psalm 147 Deuteronomy 8.2–16 1 Corinthians 10.1–17	*EP* Psalms 23, 42, 43 Proverbs 9.1–5 Luke 9.11–17

Alternatively, Corpus Christi may be kept as a Lesser Festival, and either these readings or those given below may be used.

			Holy Communion	Morning Prayer	Evening Prayer
Thursday	**3 June** Day of Thanksgiving for the Institution of the Holy Communion (Corpus Christi) *Martyrs of Uganda, 1885–7, 1977*	*G*	2 Timothy 2.8–15 Psalm 25.4–12 Mark 12.28–34	Psalms 14, **15**, 16 Joshua 8.30–end Luke 11.14–28	Psalm **18*** 2 Chronicles 29.20–end Romans 5.12–end
Friday	**4 June** *Petroc, abbot, 6th cent.*	*G*	2 Timothy 3.10–end Psalm 119.161–168 Mark 12.35–37	Psalms 17, **19** Joshua 9.3–26 Luke 11.29–36	Psalm **22** 2 Chronicles 30 Romans 6.1–14
Saturday	**5 June** Boniface (Wynfrith), bishop, martyr, 754 (see p. 72)	*Gr*	2 Timothy 4.1–8 Psalm 71.7–16 Mark 12.38–end	Psalms 20, 21, **23** Joshua 10.1–15 Luke 11.37–end	Psalms **24**, 25 2 Chronicles 32.1–22 Romans 6.15–end

			Principal Service	3rd Service	2nd Service
Sunday	**6 June** **1st Sunday after Trinity** Proper 5	*G*	*Continuous:* 1 Kings 17.8–16 [17–end] Psalm 146 *Related:* 1 Kings 17.17–end Psalm 30 Galatians 1.11–end Luke 7.11–17	Psalm 45 Deuteronomy 6.10–end Acts 22.22—23.11	Psalm 44 [44.1–9] Genesis 8.15—9.17 Mark 4.1–20
			Holy Communion	**Morning Prayer**	**Evening Prayer**
Monday	**7 June** DEL week 10	*G*	1 Kings 17.1–6 Psalm 121 Matthew 5.1–12	Psalms 27, **30** Joshua 14 Luke 12.1–12	Psalms 26, **28**, 29 2 Chronicles 33.1–13 Romans 7.1–6
Tuesday	**8 June** Thomas Ken, bishop, nonjuror, hymn writer, 1711 (see p. 74)	*Gw*	1 Kings 17.7–16 Psalm 4 Matthew 5.13–16	Psalms 32, **36** Joshua 21.43—22.8 Luke 12.13–21	Psalm **33** 2 Chronicles 34.1–18 Romans 7.7–end
Wednesday	**9 June** Columba, abbot, missionary, 597 (see p. 75) *Ephrem, deacon, hymn writer, teacher of the faith, 373*	*Gw*	1 Kings 18.20–39 Psalm 16.1, 6–end Matthew 5.17–19	Psalm **34** Joshua 22.9–end Luke 12.22–31	Psalm **119.33–56** 2 Chronicles 34.19–end Romans 8.1–11
Thursday	**10 June**	*G*	1 Kings 18.41–end Psalm 65.8–end Matthew 5.20–26	Psalm **37*** Joshua 23 Luke 12.32–40	Psalms 39, **40** 2 Chronicles 35.1–19 Romans 8.12–17 *or:* 1st EP of Barnabas the Apostle: Psalms 1, 15; Isaiah 42.5–12; Acts 14.8–end
			Principal Service	**3rd Service**	**2nd Service**
Friday	**11 June** Barnabas the Apostle	*R*	Job 29.11–16 *or* Acts 11.19–end Psalm 112 Acts 11.19–end *or* Galatians 2.1–10 John 15.12–17	*MP* Psalms 100, 101, 117 Jeremiah 9.23–24 Acts 4.32–end	*EP* Psalm 147 Ecclesiastes 12.9–end *or* Tobit 4.5–11 Acts 9.26–31
			Holy Communion	**Morning Prayer**	**Evening Prayer**
Saturday	**12 June**	*G*	1 Kings 19.19–end Psalm 16.1–7 Matthew 5.33–37	Psalms 41, **42**, 43 Joshua 24.29–end Luke 12.49–end	Psalms 45, **46** 2 Chronicles 36.11–end Romans 8.31–end

Trinity 2

		Principal Service	3rd Service	2nd Service
Sunday	**13 June** *G* **2nd Sunday after Trinity** Proper 6	*Continuous:* 1 Kings 21.1–10 [11–14] 15–21*a* Psalm 5.1–8 *Related:* 2 Samuel 11.26—12.10, 13–15 Psalm 32 Galatians 2.15–end Luke 7.36—8.3	Psalm 49 Deuteronomy 10.12—11.1 Acts 23.12–end	Psalms 52 [53] Genesis 13 Mark 4.21–end
		Holy Communion	**Morning Prayer**	**Evening Prayer**
Monday	**14 June** *G* *Richard Baxter, puritan divine, 1691* DEL week 11	1 Kings 21.1–16 Psalm 5.1–5 Matthew 5.38–42	Psalm **44** Judges 2 Luke 13.1–9	Psalms **47**, 49 Ezra 1 Romans 9.1–18
Tuesday	**15 June** *G* *Evelyn Underhill, spiritual writer, 1941*	1 Kings 21.17–end Psalm 51.1–9 Matthew 5.43–end	Psalms **48**, 52 Judges 4.1–23 Luke 13.10–21	Psalm **50** Ezra 3 Romans 9.19–end
Wednesday	**16 June** *Gw* Richard, bishop, 1253 (see p. 74) *Joseph Butler, bishop, philosopher, 1752*	2 Kings 2.1, 6–14 Psalm 31.21–end Matthew 6.1–6, 16–18	Psalm **119.57–80** Judges 5 Luke 13.22–end	Psalms **59**, 60 (67) Ezra 4.1–5 Romans 10.1–10
Thursday	**17 June** *G* *Samuel and Henrietta Barnett, social reformers, 1913 and 1936*	Ecclesiasticus 48.1–14 *or* Isaiah 63.7–9 Psalm 97.1–8 Matthew 6.7–15	Psalms 56, **57** (63*) Judges 6.1–24 Luke 14.1–11	Psalms 61, **62**, 64 Ezra 4.7–end Romans 10.11–end
Friday	**18 June** *G* *Bernard Mizeki, martyr, 1896*	2 Kings 11.1–4, 9–18, 20 Psalm 132.1–5, 11–13 Matthew 6.19–23	Psalms **51**, 54 Judges 6.25–end Luke 14.12–24	Psalm **38** Ezra 5 Romans 11.1–12
Saturday	**19 June** *G* *Sundar Singh, sadhu (holy man), evangelist, teacher of the faith, 1929*	2 Chronicles 24.17–25 Psalm 89.25–33 Matthew 6.24–end	Psalm **68** Judges 7 Luke 14.25–end	Psalms 65, **66** Ezra 6 Romans 11.13–24

			Principal Service	3rd Service	2nd Service
Sunday	**20 June** **3rd Sunday after Trinity** Proper 7	*G*	*Continuous:* 1 Kings 19.1–4 [5–7] 8–15*a* Psalms 42, 43 [42 *or* 43] *Related:* Isaiah 65.1–9 Psalm 22.19–28 Galatians 3.23–end Luke 8.26–39	Psalm 55.1–16, 18–21 Deuteronomy 11.1–15 Acts 27.1–12	Psalms [50] 57 Genesis 24.1–27 Mark 5.21–end
			Holy Communion	**Morning Prayer**	**Evening Prayer**
Monday	**21 June** DEL week 12	*G*	2 Kings 17.5–8, 13–15, 18 Psalm 60.1–5, 11–end Matthew 7.1–5	Psalm **71** Judges 8.22–end Luke 15.1–10	Psalms **72**, 75 Ezra 7 Romans 11.25–end
Tuesday	**22 June** Alban, first martyr of Britain, *c.*250 (see p. 72)	*Gr*	2 Kings 19.9*b*–11, 14–21, 31–36 Psalm 48.1–2, 8–end Matthew 7.6, 12–14	Psalm **73** Judges 9.1–21 Luke 15.11–end	Psalm **74** Ezra 8.15–end Romans 12.1–8
Wednesday	**23 June** Etheldreda, abbess, *c.*678 (see p. 75) Ember Day	*Gw*	2 Kings 22.8–13, 23.1–3 Psalm 119.33–40 Matthew 7.15–20	Psalm **77** Judges 9.22–end Luke 16.1–18	Psalm **119.81–104** Ezra 9 Romans 12.9–end *or:* 1st EP of the Birth of John the Baptist: Psalm 71; Judges 13.2–7, 24–end; Luke 1.5–25
			Principal Service	**3rd Service**	**2nd Service**
Thursday	**24 June** Birth of John the Baptist	*W*	Isaiah 40.1–11 Psalm 85.7–end Acts 13.14*b*–26 *or* Galatians 3.23–end Luke 1.57–66, 80	*MP* Psalms 50, 149 Ecclesiasticus 48.1–10 *or* Malachi 3.1–6 Luke 3.1–17	*EP* Psalms 80, 82 Malachi 4 Matthew 11.2–19
			Holy Communion	**Morning Prayer**	**Evening Prayer**
Friday	**25 June** Ember Day	*G*	2 Kings 25.1–12 Psalm 137.1–6 Matthew 8.1–4	Psalm **55** Judges 11.29–end Luke 17.1–10	Psalm **69** Nehemiah 1 Romans 13.8–end
Saturday	**26 June** Ember Day	*G*	Lamentations 2.2, 10–14, 18–19 Psalm 74.1–3, 21–end Matthew 8.5–17	Psalms **76**, 79 Judges 12.1–7 Luke 17.11–19	Psalms 81, **84** Nehemiah 2 Romans 14.1–12

Trinity 4

		Principal Service	3rd Service	2nd Service
Sunday	**27 June** *G* **4th Sunday after Trinity** Proper 8	*Continuous:* 2 Kings 2.1–2, 6–14 Psalm 77.1–2, 11–end [77.11–end] *Related:* 1 Kings 19.15–16, 19–end Psalm 16 Galatians 5.1, 13–25 Luke 9.51–end	Psalm 64 Deuteronomy 15.1–11 Acts 27.[13–32] 33–end	Psalms [59.1–6, 18–end] 60 Genesis 27.1–40 Mark 6.1–6

		Holy Communion	Morning Prayer	Evening Prayer
Monday	**28 June** *Gw* Irenaeus, bishop, teacher of the faith, *c.*200 (see p. 73) DEL week 13	Amos 2.6–10, 13–end Psalm 50.16–23 Matthew 8.18–22	Psalms **80**, 82 Judges 13.1–24 Luke 17.20–end	Psalms **85**, 86 Nehemiah 4 Romans 14.13–end *or:* 1st EP of Peter and Paul, Apostles [*or* Peter the Apostle alone†]: Psalms 66, 67; Ezekiel 3.4–11; Galatians 1.13—2.8 [†Acts 9.32–end]

		Principal Service	3rd Service	2nd Service
Tuesday	**29 June** *R* Peter and Paul, Apostles *or* Peter the Apostle	*Peter and Paul:* Zechariah 4.1–6*a*, 10*b*–end *or* Acts 12.1–11 Psalm 125 Acts 12.1–11 *or* 2 Timothy 4.6–8, 17–18 Matthew 16.13–19 *Peter alone:* Ezekiel 3.22–end *or* Acts 12.1–11 Psalm 125 Acts 12.1–11 *or* 1 Peter 2.19–end Matthew 16.13–19	*MP* Psalms 71, 113 Isaiah 49.1–6 Acts 11.1–18	*EP* Psalms 124, 138 Ezekiel 34.11–16 John 21.15–22

		Holy Communion	Morning Prayer	Evening Prayer
Wednesday	**30 June** *G*	Amos 5.14–15, 21–24 Psalm 50.7–14 Matthew 8.28–end	Psalm **119.105–128** Judges 15.1—16.3 Luke 18.15–30	Psalms **91**, 93 Nehemiah 6.1—7.4 Romans 15.14–21
Thursday	**1 July** *G* *Henry, John and Henry Venn, priests, evangelical divines, 1797, 1813, 1873*	Amos 7.10–end Psalm 19.7–10 Matthew 9.1–8	Psalms 90, **92** Judges 16.4–end Luke 18.31–end	Psalm **94** Nehemiah 7.73*b*—end of 8 Romans 15.22–end
Friday	**2 July** *G*	Amos 8.4–6, 9–12 Psalm 119.1–8 Matthew 9.9–13	Psalms **88** (95) Judges 17 Luke 19.1–10	Psalm **102** Nehemiah 9.1–23 Romans 16.1–16 *or:* 1st EP of Thomas the Apostle: Psalm 27; Isaiah 35; Hebrews 10.35—11.1

		Principal Service	3rd Service	2nd Service
Saturday	**3 July** *R* Thomas the Apostle	Habakkuk 2.1–4 Psalm 31.1–6 Ephesians 2.19–end John 20.24–29	*MP* Psalms 92, 146 2 Samuel 15.17–21 *or* Ecclesiasticus 2 John 11.1–16	*EP* Psalm 139 Job 42.1–6 1 Peter 1.3–12

			Principal Service	3rd Service	2nd Service
Sunday	**4 July** **5th Sunday after Trinity** Proper 9	*G*	*Continuous:* 2 Kings 5.1–14 Psalm 30 *Related:* Isaiah 66.10–14 Psalm 66.1–8 Galatians 6.[1–6] 7–16 Luke 10.1–11, 16–20	Psalm 74 Deuteronomy 24.10–end Acts 28.1–16	Psalm 65 [70] Genesis 29.1–20 Mark 6.7–29
			Holy Communion	**Morning Prayer**	**Evening Prayer**
Monday	**5 July** DEL week 14	*G*	Hosea 2.14–16, 19–20 Psalm 145.2–9 Matthew 9.18–26	Psalms **98**, 99, 101 1 Samuel 1.1–20 Luke 19.28–40	Psalm **105*** (*or* 103) Nehemiah 12.27–47 2 Corinthians 1.1–14
Tuesday	**6 July** *Thomas More, scholar, and John Fisher, bishop, martyrs, 1535*	*G*	Hosea 8.4–7, 11–13 Psalm 103.8–12 Matthew 9.32–end	Psalm **106*** (*or* 103) 1 Samuel 1.21—2.11 Luke 19.41–end	Psalm **107*** Nehemiah 13.1–14 2 Corinthians 1.15—2.4
Wednesday	**7 July**	*G*	Hosea 10.1–3, 7–8, 12 Psalm 115.3–10 Matthew 10.1–7	Psalms 110, **111**, 112 1 Samuel 2.12–26 Luke 20.1–8	Psalm **119.129–152** Nehemiah 13.15–end 2 Corinthians 2.5–end
Thursday	**8 July**	*G*	Hosea 11.1, 3–4, 8–9 Psalm 105.1–7 Matthew 10.7–15	Psalms 113, **115** 1 Samuel 2.27–end Luke 20.9–19	Psalms 114, **116**, 117 Esther 1 2 Corinthians 3
Friday	**9 July**	*G*	Hosea 14.2–end Psalm 80.1–7 Matthew 10.16–23	Psalm **139** 1 Samuel 3.1—4.1*a* Luke 20.20–26	Psalms **130**, 131, 137 Esther 2 2 Corinthians 4
Saturday	**10 July**	*G*	Isaiah 6.1–8 Psalm 51.1–7 Matthew 10.24–33	Psalms 120, **121**, 122 1 Samuel 4.1*b*–end Luke 20.27–40	Psalm **118** Esther 3 2 Corinthians 5

Trinity 6

				Principal Service	3rd Service	2nd Service
Sunday	**11 July** **6th Sunday after Trinity** Proper 10	*G*	*Continuous:* Amos 7.7–end Psalm 82	*Related:* Deuteronomy 30.9–14 Psalm 25.1–10	Psalm 76 Deuteronomy 28.1–14 Acts 28.17–end	Psalm 77 [77.1–12] Genesis 32.9–30 Mark 7.1–23
			Colossians 1.1–14 Luke 10.25–37			

			Holy Communion	Morning Prayer	Evening Prayer
Monday	**12 July** DEL week 15	*G*	Isaiah 1.11–17 Psalm 50.7–15 Matthew 10.34—11.1	Psalms 123, 124, 125, **126** 1 Samuel 5 Luke 20.41—21.4	Psalms **127**, 128, 129 Esther 4 2 Corinthians 6.1—7.1
Tuesday	**13 July**	*G*	Isaiah 7.1–9 Psalm 48.1–7 1 Matthew 11.20–24	Psalms **132**, 133 Samuel 6.1–16 Luke 21.5–19	Psalms (134), **135** Esther 5 2 Corinthians 7.2–end
Wednesday	**14 July** John Keble, priest, poet, 1866 (see p. 74)	*Gw*	Isaiah 10.5–7, 13–16 Psalm 94.5–11 Matthew 11.25–27	Psalm **119.153–end** 1 Samuel 7 Luke 21.20–28	Psalm **136** Esther 6.1–13 2 Corinthians 8.1–15
Thursday	**15 July** Swithun, bishop, *c.*862 (see p. 74) *Bonaventure, friar, bishop, teacher of the faith, 1274*	*Gw*	Isaiah 26.7–9, 16–19 Psalm 102.14–21 Matthew 11.28–end	Psalms **143**, 146 1 Samuel 8 Luke 21.29–end	Psalms **138**, 140, 141 Esther 6.14—end of 7 2 Corinthians 8.16—9.5
Friday	**16 July** *Osmund, bishop, 1099*	*G*	Isaiah 38.1–6, 21–22, 7–8 [*sic*] *Canticle:* Isaiah 38.10–16 *or* Psalm 32.1–8 Matthew 12.1–8	Psalms 142, **144** 1 Samuel 9.1–14 Luke 22.1–13	Psalm **145** Esther 8 2 Corinthians 9.6–end
Saturday	**17 July**	*G*	Micah 2.1–5 Psalm 10.1–5*a*, 12 Matthew 12.14–21	Psalm **147** 1 Samuel 9.15—10.1 Luke 22.14–23	Psalms **148**, 149, 150 Esther 9.20–28 2 Corinthians 10

		Principal Service	3rd Service	2nd Service
Sunday	**18 July** *G* **7th Sunday after Trinity** Proper 11	*Continuous:* Amos 8.1–12 Psalm 52 *Related:* Genesis 18.1–10*a* Psalm 15 Colossians 1.15–28 Luke 10.38–end	Psalms 82, 100 Deuteronomy 30.1–10 1 Peter 3.8–18	Psalm 81 Genesis 41.1–16, 25–37 1 Corinthians 4.8–13 *HC* John 4.31–35

		Holy Communion	Morning Prayer	Evening Prayer
Monday	**19 July** *Gw* Gregory, bishop, and his sister Macrina, deaconess, teachers of the faith, *c.*394 and *c.*379 (see p. 73) DEL week 16	Micah 6.1–4, 6–8 Psalm 50.3–7, 14 Matthew 12.38–42	Psalms **1**, 2, 3 1 Samuel 10.1–16 Luke 22.24–30	Psalms **4**, 7 Jeremiah 26 2 Corinthians 11.1–15
Tuesday	**20 July** *G* *Margaret of Antioch, martyr, 4th cent.* *Bartolomé de las Casas, Apostle to the Indies, 1566*	Micah 7.14–15, 18–20 Psalm 85.1–7 Matthew 12.46–end	Psalms **5**, 6 (8) 1 Samuel 10.17–end Luke 22.31–38	Psalms **9**, 10* Jeremiah 28 2 Corinthians 11.16–end
Wednesday	**21 July** *G*	Jeremiah 1.1, 4–10 Psalm 70 Matthew 13.1–9	Psalm **119.1–32** 1 Samuel 11 Luke 22.39–46	Psalms **11**, 12, 13 Jeremiah 29.1–14 2 Corinthians 12 *or:* 1st EP of Mary Magdalene: Psalm 139; Isaiah 25.1–9; 2 Corinthians 1.3–7

			Principal Service	3rd Service	2nd Service
Thursday	**22 July** Mary Magdalene	*W*	Song of Solomon 3.1–4 Psalm 42.1–10 2 Corinthians 5.14–17 John 20.1–2, 11–18	*MP* Psalms 30, 32, 150 1 Samuel 16.14–end Luke 8.1–3	*EP* Psalm 63 Zephaniah 3.14–end Mark 15.40—16.7
			Holy Communion	**Morning Prayer**	**Evening Prayer**
Friday	**23 July** *Bridget, abbess, 1373*	*G*	Jeremiah 3.14–17 Psalm 23 *or Canticle:* Jeremiah 31.10–13 Matthew 13.18–23	Psalms 17, **19** 1 Samuel 13.5–18 Luke 22.63–end	Psalm **22** Jeremiah 30.12–22 James 1.1–11
Saturday	**24 July**	*G*	Jeremiah 7.1–11 Psalm 84.1–6 Matthew 13.24–30	Psalms 20, 21, **23** 1 Samuel 13.19—14.15 Luke 23.1–12	Psalms **24**, 25 Jeremiah 31.1–22 James 1.12–end *or:* 1st EP of James the Apostle: Psalm 144; Deuteronomy 30.11–end; Mark 5.2–end

James / Trinity 8

If St James is celebrated on Sunday 25 July:

			Principal Service	3rd Service	2nd Service
Sunday	**25 July** James the Apostle	*R*	Jeremiah 45.1–5 *or* Acts 11.27—12.2 Psalm 126 Acts 11.27—12.2 *or* 2 Corinthians 4.7–15 Matthew 20.20–28	*MP* Psalms 7, 29, 117 2 Kings 1.9–15 Luke 9.46–56	*EP* Psalm 94 Jeremiah 26.1–15 Mark 1.14–20

			Holy Communion	Morning Prayer	Evening Prayer
Monday	**26 July** Anne and Joachim, parents of the Blessed Virgin Mary DEL week 17	*Gw*	Jeremiah 13.1–11 Psalm 82 *or* Deuteronomy 32.18–21 Matthew 13.31–35 *Lesser Festival eucharistic lectionary:* Zephaniah 3.14–18*a*; Psalm 127; Romans 8.28–30; Matthew 13.16–17	Psalms 27, **30** 1 Samuel 14.24–46 Luke 23.13–25	Psalms 26, **28**, 29 Jeremiah 31.23–25, 27–37 James 2.1–13

If St James is celebrated on Monday 26 July:

			Principal Service	3rd Service	2nd Service
Sunday	**25 July** **8th Sunday after Trinity** Proper 12	*G*	*Continuous:* Hosea 1.2–10; Psalm 85 [85.1–7] *Related:* Genesis 18.20–32; Psalm 138 Colossians 2.6–15 [16–19] Luke 11.1–13	Psalm 95 Song of Solomon 2 *or* 1 Maccabees 2.[1–14] 15–22 1 Peter 4.7–14	Psalm 88 [88.1–10] Genesis 42.1–25 1 Corinthians 10.1–24 *HC* Matthew 13.24–30 [31–43] *or:* 1st EP of James the Apostle: Psalm 144; Deuteronomy 30.11–end; Mark 5.21–end
Monday	**26 July** James the Apostle (transferred from 25 July)	*R*	Jeremiah 45.1–5 *or* Acts 11.27—12.2 Psalm 126 Acts 11.27—12.2 *or* 2 Corinthians 4.7–15 Matthew 20.20–28	*MP* Psalms 7, 29, 117 2 Kings 1.9–15 Luke 9.46–56	*EP* Psalm 94 Jeremiah 26.1–15 Mark 1.14–20

Trinity 8

			Holy Communion	Morning Prayer	Evening Prayer
Tuesday	**27 July** *Brooke Foss Westcott, bishop, teacher of the faith, 1901*	*G*	Jeremiah 14.17–end Psalm 79.8–end Matthew 13.36–43	Psalms 32, **36** 1 Samuel 15.1–23 Luke 23.26–43	Psalm **33** Jeremiah 32.1–15 James 2.14–end
Wednesday	**28 July**	*G*	Jeremiah 15.10, 16–end Psalm 59.1–4, 18–end Matthew 13.44–46	Psalm **34** 1 Samuel 16 Luke 23.44–56*a*	Psalm **119.33–56** Jeremiah 33.1–13 James 3
Thursday	**29 July** Mary, Martha and Lazarus, companions of Our Lord	*Gw*	Jeremiah 18.1–6 Psalm 146.1–5 Matthew 13.47–53 *Lesser Festival eucharistic lectionary:* Isaiah 25.6–9; Psalm 49.5–10, 16; Hebrews 2.10–15; John 12.1–8	Psalm **37*** 1 Samuel 17.1–30 Luke 23.56*b*–24.12	Psalms 39, **40** Jeremiah 33.14–end James 4.1–12
Friday	**30 July** William Wilberforce, social reformer, 1833 (see p. 76)	*Gw*	Jeremiah 26.1–9 Psalm 69.4–10 Matthew 13.54–end	Psalm **31** 1 Samuel 17.31–54 Luke 24.13–35	Psalm **35** Jeremiah 35 James 4.13—5.6
Saturday	**31 July** *Ignatius of Loyola, founder of the Society of Jesus, 1556*	*G*	Jeremiah 26.11–16, 24 Psalm 69.14–20 Matthew 14.1–12	Psalms 41, **42**, 43 1 Samuel 17.55—18.16 Luke 24.36–end	Psalms 45, **46** Jeremiah 36.1–18 James 5.7–end

			Principal Service	3rd Service	2nd Service
Sunday	**1 August** **9th Sunday after Trinity** Proper 13	*G*	*Continuous:* Hosea 11.1–11 Psalm 107.1–9, 43 [107.1–9] *Related:* Ecclesiastes 1.2, 12–14; 2.18–23 Psalm 49.1–12 [49.1–9] Colossians 3.1–11 Luke 12.13–21	Psalm 106.1–10 Song of Solomon 5.2–end *or* 1 Maccabees 3.1–12 2 Peter 1.1–15	Psalm 107.1–32 [107.1–12] Genesis 50.4–end 1 Corinthians 14.1–19 *HC* Mark 6.45–52

			Holy Communion	Morning Prayer	Evening Prayer
Monday	**2 August** DEL week 18	*G*	Jeremiah 28 Psalm 119.89–96 Matthew 14.13–21 *or* 14.22–end	Psalm **44** 1 Samuel 19.1–18 Acts 1.1–14	Psalms **47**, 49 Jeremiah 36.19–end Mark 1.1–1
Tuesday	**3 August**	*G*	Jeremiah 30.1–2, 12–15, 18–22 Psalm 102.16–21 Matthew 14.22–end *or* 15.1–2, 10–14	Psalms **48**, 52 1 Samuel 20.1–17 Acts 1.15–end	Psalm **50** Jeremiah 37 Mark 1.14–20
Wednesday	**4 August** *Jean-Baptiste Vianney, curé d'Ars, spiritual guide, 1859*	*G*	Jeremiah 31.1–7 Psalm 121 Matthew 15.21–28	Psalm **119.57–80** 1 Samuel 20.18–end Acts 2.1–21	Psalms **59**, 60 (67) Jeremiah 38.1–13 Mark 1.21–28
Thursday	**5 August** Oswald, king, martyr, 642 (see p. 72)	*Gr*	Jeremiah 31.31–34 Psalm 51.11–18 Matthew 16.13–23	Psalms 56, **57** (63*) 1 Samuel 21.1—22.5 Acts 2.22–36	Psalms 61, **62**, 64 Jeremiah 38.14–end Mark 1.29–end *or:* 1st EP of the Transfiguration of Our Lord: Psalms 99, 110; Exodus 24.12–end; John 12.27–36*a*

			Principal Service	3rd Service	2nd Service
Friday	**6 August** Transfiguration of Our Lord	*W*	Daniel 7.9–10, 13–14 Psalm 97 2 Peter 1.16–19 Luke 9.28–36	*MP* Psalms 27, 150 Ecclesiasticus 48.1–10 *or* 1 Kings 19.1–16 1 John 3.1–3	*EP* Psalm 72 Exodus 34.29–end 2 Corinthians 3

			Holy Communion	Morning Prayer	Evening Prayer
Saturday	**7 August** *John Mason Neale, priest, hymn writer, 1866*	*G*	Habakkuk 1.12—2.4 Psalm 9.7–11 Matthew 17.14–20	Psalm **68** 1 Samuel 23 Acts 3.1–10	Psalms 65, **66** Jeremiah 40 Mark 2.13–22

Trinity 10

		Principal Service	3rd Service	2nd Service
Sunday	**8 August** *G* **10th Sunday after Trinity** Proper 14	*Continuous:* Isaiah 1.1, 10–20 Psalm 50.1–8, 23–end [50.1–7] *Related:* Genesis 15.1–6 Psalm 33.12–end [33.12–21] Hebrews 11.1–3, 8–16 Luke 12.32–40	Psalm 115 Song of Solomon 8.5–7 *or* 1 Maccabees 14.4–15 2 Peter 3.8–13	Psalms 108 [116] Isaiah 11.10—end of 12 2 Corinthians 1.1–22 *HC* Mark 7.24–30
		Holy Communion	**Morning Prayer**	**Evening Prayer**
Monday	**9 August** *Gw* Mary Sumner, founder of the Mothers' Union, 1921 (see p. 76) DEL week 19	Ezekiel 1.2–5, 24–end Psalm 148.1–4, 12–13 Matthew 17.22–end	Psalm **71** 1 Samuel 24 Acts 3.11–end	Psalms **72**, 75 Jeremiah 41 Mark 2.23—3.6
Tuesday	**10 August** *Gr* Laurence, deacon, martyr, 258 (see p. 72)	Ezekiel 2.8—3.4 Psalm 119.65–72 Matthew 18.1–5, 10, 12–14	Psalm **73** 1 Samuel 26 Acts 4.1–12	Psalm **74** Jeremiah 42 Mark 3.7–19*a*
Wednesday	**11 August** *Gw* Clare of Assisi, founder of the Poor Clares, 1253 (see p. 75) *John Henry Newman, priest, 1890*	Ezekiel 9.1–7, 10, 18–22 Psalm 113 Matthew 18.15–20	Psalm **77** 1 Samuel 28.3–end Acts 4.13–31	Psalm **119.81–104** Jeremiah 43 Mark 3.19*b*–end
Thursday	**12 August** *G*	Ezekiel 12.1–12 Psalm 78.58–64 Matthew 18.21—19.1	Psalm **78.1–39*** 1 Samuel 31 Acts 4.32—5.11	Psalm **78.40–end*** Jeremiah 44.1–14 Mark 4.1–20
Friday	**13 August** *Gw* Jeremy Taylor, bishop, teacher of the faith, 1667 (see p. 73) *Florence Nightingale, nurse, social reformer, 1910* *Octavia Hill, social reformer, 1912*	Ezekiel 16.1–15, 60–end Psalm 118.14–18 *or Canticle:* Song of Deliverance Matthew 19.3–12	Psalm **55** 2 Samuel 1 Acts 5.12–26	Psalm **69** Jeremiah 44.15–end Mark 4.21–34
Saturday	**14 August** *G* *Maximilian Kolbe, friar, martyr, 1941*	Ezekiel 18.1–11*a*, 13*b*, 30, 32 Psalm 51.1–3, 15–17 Matthew 19.13–15	Psalms **76**, 79 2 Samuel 2.1–11 Acts 5.27–end	Psalms 81, **84** Jeremiah 45 Mark 4.35–end *or:* 1st EP of the Blessed Virgin Mary: Psalm 72; Proverbs 8.22–31; John 19.23–27

Blessed Virgin Mary / Trinity 11

If the Blessed Virgin Mary is celebrated on Sunday 15 August:

		Principal Service	3rd Service	2nd Service
Sunday	**15 August** *W* The Blessed Virgin Mary	Isaiah 61.10–end *or* Revelation 11.19—12.6, 10 Psalm 45.10–end Galatians 4.4–7 Luke 1.46–55	*MP* Psalms 98, 138, 147.1–12 Isaiah 7.10–15 Luke 11.27–28	*EP* Psalm 132 Song of Solomon 2.1–7 Acts 1.6–14

		Holy Communion	Morning Prayer	Evening Prayer
Monday	**16 August** *G* DEL week 20	Ezekiel 24.15–24 Psalm 78.1–8 Matthew 19.16–22	Psalms **80**, 82 2 Samuel 3.12–end Acts 6	Psalms **85**, 86 Micah 1.1–9 Mark 5.1–20

If the Blessed Virgin Mary is celebrated on Monday 16 August or Wednesday 8 September:

		Principal Service	3rd Service	2nd Service
Sunday	**15 August** *G* **11th Sunday after Trinity** Proper 15	*Continuous:* Isaiah 5.1–7; Psalm 80.[1–2] 9–end *Related:* Jeremiah 23.23–29; Psalm 82 Hebrews 11.29—12.2 Luke 12.49–56	Psalm 119.33–48 Jonah 1 *or* Ecclesiasticus 3.1–15 2 Peter 3.14–end	Psalm 119.17–32 [119.17–24] Isaiah 28.9–22 2 Corinthians 8.1–9 *HC* Matthew 20.1–16 *or:* 1st EP of the Blessed Virgin Mary: Psalm 72; Proverbs 8.22–31; John 19.23–27
Monday	**16 August** *W* The Blessed Virgin Mary (transferred from 15 August)	Isaiah 61.10–end *or* Revelation 11.19—12.6, 10 Psalm 45.10–end Galatians 4.4–7 Luke 1.46–55	*MP* Psalms 98, 138, 147.1–12 Isaiah 7.10–15 Luke 11.27–28	*EP* Psalm 132 Song of Solomon 2.1–7 Acts 1.6–14

			Holy Communion	Morning Prayer	Evening Prayer
Tuesday	**17 August**	*G*	Ezekiel 28.1–10 Psalm 107.1–3, 40, 43 Matthew 19.23–end	Psalms 87, **89.1–18** 2 Samuel 5.1–12 Acts 7.1–16	Psalm **89.19–end** Micah 2 Mark 5.21–34
Wednesday	**18 August**	*G*	Ezekiel 34.1–11 Psalm 23 Matthew 20.1–16	Psalm **119.105–128** 2 Samuel 6.1–19 Acts 7.17–43	Psalms **91**, 93 Micah 3 Mark 5.35–end
Thursday	**19 August**	*G*	Ezekiel 36.23–28 Psalm 51.7–12 Matthew 22.1–14	Psalms 90, **92** 2 Samuel 7.1–17 Acts 7.44–53	Psalm **94** Micah 4.1—5.1 Mark 6.1–13
Friday	**20 August** Bernard, abbot, teacher of the faith, 1153 (see p. 73) *William and Catherine Booth, founders of the Salvation Army, 1912, 1890*	*Gw*	Ezekiel 37.1–14 Psalm 107.1–8 Matthew 22.34–40	Psalms **88** (95) 2 Samuel 7.18–end Acts 7.54—8.3	Psalm **102** Micah 5.2–end Mark 6.14–29
Saturday	**21 August**	*G*	Ezekiel 43.1–7 Psalm 85.7–end Matthew 23.1–12	Psalms 96, **97**, 100 2 Samuel 9 Acts 8.4–25	Psalm **104** Micah 6 Mark 6.30–44

Day	Date	Principal Service	3rd Service	2nd Service
Sunday	**22 August** *G* **12th Sunday after Trinity** Proper 16	*Continuous:* Jeremiah 1.4–10; Psalm 71.1–6 *Related:* Isaiah 58.9*b*–end; Psalm 103.1–8 Hebrews 12.18–end Luke 13.10–17	Psalm 119.73–88 Jonah 2 *or* Ecclesiasticus 3.17–29 Revelation 1	Psalm 119.49–72 [119.49–56] Isaiah 30.8–21 2 Corinthians 9 *HC* Matthew 21.28–32
		Holy Communion	**Morning Prayer**	**Evening Prayer**
Monday	**23 August** *G* DEL week 21	2 Thessalonians 1.1–5, 11–end Psalm 39.1–9 Matthew 23.13–22	Psalms **98**, 99, 101 2 Samuel 11 Acts 8.26–end	Psalm **105*** (*or* 103) Micah 7.1–7 Mark 6.45–end *or:* 1st EP of Bartholomew the Apostle: Psalm 97; Isaiah 61.1–9; 2 Corinthians 6.1–10
		Principal Service	**3rd Service**	**2nd Service**
Tuesday	**24 August** *R* Bartholomew the Apostle	Isaiah 43.8–13 *or* Acts 5.12–16 Psalm 145.1–7 Acts 5.12–16 *or* 1 Corinthians 4.9–15 Luke 22.24–30	*MP* Psalms 86, 117 Genesis 28.10–17 John 1.43–end Matthew 10.1–22	*EP* Psalms 91, 116 Ecclesiasticus 39.1–10 *or* Deuteronomy 18.15–19
		Holy Communion	**Morning Prayer**	**Evening Prayer**
Wednesday	**25 August** *G*	2 Thessalonians 3.6–10, 16–end Psalm 128 Matthew 23.27–32	Psalms 110, **111**, 112 2 Samuel 15.1–12 Acts 9.19*b*–31	Psalm **119.129–152** Habakkuk 1.1–11 Mark 7.14–23
Thursday	**26 August** *G*	1 Corinthians 1.1–9 Psalm 145.1–7 Matthew 24.42–end	Psalms 113, **115** 2 Samuel 15.13–end Acts 9.32–end	Psalms 114, **116**, 117 Habakkuk 1.12—2.5 Mark 7.24–30
Friday	**27 August** *Gw* Monica, mother of Augustine of Hippo, 387 (see p. 76)	1 Corinthians 1.17–25 Psalm 33.6–12 Matthew 25.1–13	Psalm **139** 2 Samuel 16.1–14 Acts 10.1–16	Psalms **130**, 131, 137 Habakkuk 2.6–end Mark 7.31–end
Saturday	**28 August** *Gw* Augustine, bishop, teacher of the faith, 430 (see p. 73)	1 Corinthians 1.26–end Psalm 33.12–15, 20–end Matthew 25.14–30	Psalms 120, **121**, 122 2 Samuel 17.1–23 Acts 10.17–33	Psalm **118** Habakkuk 3.2–19*a* Mark 8.1–10

Trinity 13

		Principal Service	3rd Service	2nd Service
Sunday	**29 August** *G* **13th Sunday after Trinity** Proper 17	*Continuous:* Jeremiah 2.4–13 Psalm 81.1, 10–end [81.1–11] *Related:* Ecclesiasticus 10.12–18 *or* Proverbs 25.6–7 Psalm 112 Hebrews 13.1–8, 15–16 Luke 14.1, 7–14	Psalm 119.161–end Jonah 3.1–9 *or* Ecclesiasticus 11.[7–17] 18–28 Revelation 3.14–22	Psalm 119.81–96 [119.81–88] Isaiah 33.13–22 John 3.22–36
		Holy Communion	**Morning Prayer**	**Evening Prayer**
Monday	**30 August** *Gw* John Bunyan, spiritual writer, 1688 (see p. 73) DEL week 22	1 Corinthians 2.1–5 Psalm 33.12–21 Luke 4.16–30	Psalms 123, 124, 125, **126** 2 Samuel 18.1–18 Acts 10.34–end	Psalms **127**, 128, 129 Haggai 1.1–11 Mark 8.11–21
Tuesday	**31 August** *Gw* Aidan, bishop, missionary, 651 (see p. 75)	1 Corinthians 2.10*b*–end Psalm 145.10–17 Luke 4.31–37	Psalms **132**, 133 2 Samuel 18.19—19.8*a* Acts 11.1–18	Psalms (134), **135** Haggai 1.12—2.9 Mark 8.22–26
Wednesday	**1 September** *G* *Giles, hermit, c.710*	1 Corinthians 3.1–9 Psalm 62 Luke 4.38–end	Psalm **119.153–end** 2 Samuel 19.8*b*–23 Acts 11.19–end	Psalm **136** Haggai 2.10–end Mark 8.27—9.1
Thursday	**2 September** *G* *Martyrs of Papua New Guinea, 1901, 1942*	1 Corinthians 3.18–end Psalm 24.1–6 Luke 5.1–11	Psalms **143**, 146 2 Samuel 19.24–end Acts 12.1–17	Psalms **138**, 140, 141 Zechariah 1.1–17 Mark 9.2–13
Friday	**3 September** *Gw* Gregory the Great, bishop, teacher of the faith, 604 (see p. 73)	1 Corinthians 4.1–5 Psalm 37.3–8 Luke 5.33–end	Psalms 142, **144** 2 Samuel 23.1–7 Acts 12.18–end	Psalm **145** Zechariah 1.18—end of 2 Mark 9.14–29
Saturday	**4 September** *G* *Birinus, bishop, 650*	1 Corinthians 4.6–15 Psalm 145.18–end Luke 6.1–5	Psalm **147** 2 Samuel 24 Acts 13.1–12	Psalms **148**, 149, 150 Zechariah 3 Mark 9.30–37

		Principal Service		3rd Service	2nd Service
Sunday	**5 September** *G* **14th Sunday after Trinity** Proper 18	*Continuous:* Jeremiah 18.1–11 Psalm 139.1–5, 12–18 [139.1–7] Philemon 1–21 Luke 14.25–33	*Related:* Deuteronomy 30.15–end Psalm 1	Psalms 122, 123 Jonah 3.10—end of 4 *or* Ecclesiasticus 27.30—28.9 Revelation 8.1–5	Psalms [120] 121 Isaiah 43.14—44.5 *HC* John 5.30–47

		Holy Communion	Morning Prayer	Evening Prayer
Monday	**6 September** *G* *Allen Gardiner, missionary, founder of the South American Mission Society, 1851* DEL week 23	1 Corinthians 5.1–8 Psalm 5.5–9a Luke 6.6–11	Psalms **1**, 2, 3 1 Kings 1.5–31 Acts 13.13–43	Psalms **4**, 7 Zechariah 4 Mark 9.38–end
Tuesday	**7 September** *G*	1 Corinthians 6.1–11 Psalm 149.1–5 Luke 6.12–19	Psalms **5**, 6 (8) 1 Kings 1.32—2.4; 2.10–12 Acts 13.44—14.7	Psalms **9**, 10* Zechariah 6.9–end Mark 10.1–16
Wednesday	**8 September** *Gw* Birth of the Blessed Virgin Mary (see p. 72)	1 Corinthians 7.25–31 Psalm 45.11–end Luke 6.20–26	Psalm **119.1–32** 1 Kings 3 Acts 14.8–end	Psalms **11**, 12, 13 Zechariah 7 Mark 10.17–31
	If the feast of the Blessed Virgin Mary *is transferred to 8 September, use the provision (including 1st EP) for 15 August.*			
Thursday	**9 September** *G* *Charles Fuge Lowder, priest, 1880*	1 Corinthians 8.1–7, 11–end Psalm 139.1–9 Luke 6.27–38	Psalms 14, **15**, 16 1 Kings 4.29—5.12 Acts 15.1–21	Psalm **18*** Zechariah 8.1–8 Mark 10.32–34
Friday	**10 September** *G*	1 Corinthians 9.16–19, 22–end Psalm 84.1–6 Luke 6.39–42	Psalms 17, **19** 1 Kings 6.1, 11–28 Acts 15.22–35	Psalm **22** Zechariah 8.9–end Mark 10.35–45
Saturday	**11 September** *G*	1 Corinthians 10.14–22 Psalm 116.10–end Luke 6.43–end	Psalms 20, 21, **23** 1 Kings 8.1–30 Acts 15.36—16.5	Psalms **24**, 25 Zechariah 9.1–12 Mark 10.46–end

Trinity 15

		Principal Service	3rd Service	2nd Service
Sunday	**12 September** *G* **15th Sunday after Trinity** Proper 19	*Continuous:* Jeremiah 4.11–12, 22–28 Psalm 14 *Related:* Exodus 32.7–14 Psalm 51.1–11 1 Timothy 1.12–17 Luke 15.1–10	Psalms 126, 127 Isaiah 44.24—45.8 Revelation 12.1–12	Psalms 124, 125 Isaiah 60 John 6.51–69

		Holy Communion	Morning Prayer	Evening Prayer
Monday	**13 September** *Gw* John Chrysostom, bishop, teacher of the faith, 407 (see p. 73) DEL week 24	1 Corinthians 11.17–26, 33 Psalm 40.7–11 Luke 7.1–10	Psalms 27, **30** 1 Kings 8.31–62 Acts 16.6–24	Psalms 26, **28**, 29 Zechariah 10 Mark 11.1–11 *or:* 1st EP of Holy Cross Day: Psalm 66; Isaiah 52.13—end of 53; Ephesians 2.11–end

		Principal Service	3rd Service	2nd Service
Tuesday	**14 September** *R* Holy Cross Day	Numbers 21.4–9 Psalm 22.23–28 Philippians 2.6–11 John 3.13–17	*MP* Psalms 2, 8, 146 Genesis 3.1–15 John 12.27–36*a*	*EP* Psalms 110, 150 Isaiah 63.1–16 1 Corinthians 1.18–25

		Holy Communion	Morning Prayer	Evening Prayer
Wednesday	**15 September** *Gr* Cyprian, bishop, martyr, 258 (see p. 72)	1 Corinthians 12.31*b*—end of 13 Psalm 33.1–12 Luke 7.31–35	Psalm **34** 1 Kings 10.1–25 Acts 17.1–15	Psalm **119.33–56** Zechariah 12.1–10 Mark 11.27–end
Thursday	**16 September** *Gw* Ninian, bishop, apostle of the Picts c.432 (see p. 75) *Edward Bouverie Pusey, priest, 1882*	1 Corinthians 15.1–11 Psalm 118.1–2, 17–20 Luke 7.36–end	Psalm **37*** 1 Kings 11.1–13 Acts 17.16–end	Psalms 39, **40** Zechariah 13 Mark 12.1–12
Friday	**17 September** *Gw* Hildegard, abbess, visionary, 1179 (see p. 75)	1 Corinthians 15.12–20 Psalm 17.1–8 Luke 8.1–3	Psalm **31** 1 Kings 11.26–end Acts 18.1–21	Psalm **35** Zechariah 14.1–11 Mark 12.13–17
Saturday	**18 September** *G*	1 Corinthians 15.35–37, 42–49 Psalm 30.1–5 Luke 8.4–15	Psalms 41, **42**, 43 1 Kings 12.1–24 Acts 18.22—19.7	Psalms 45, **46** Zechariah 14.12–end Mark 12.18–27

		Principal Service	3rd Service	2nd Service
Sunday	**19 September** *G* **16th Sunday after Trinity** Proper 20	*Continuous:* Jeremiah 8.18—9.1 Psalm 79.1–9 *Related:* Amos 8.4–7 Psalm 113 1 Timothy 2.1–7 Luke 16.1–13	Psalms 130, 131 Isaiah 45.9–22 Revelation 14.1–5	Psalm [128] 129 Ezra 1 John 7.14–36
		Holy Communion	**Morning Prayer**	**Evening Prayer**
Monday	**20 September** *Gr* John Coleridge Patteson, bishop, and companions, martyrs, 1871 (see p. 72) DEL week 25	Proverbs 3.27–34 Psalm 15 Luke 8.16–18	Psalm **44** 1 Kings 12.25—13.10 Acts 19.8–20	Psalms **47**, 49 Ecclesiasticus 1.1–10 *or* Ezekiel 1.1–14 Mark 12.28–34 *or:* 1st EP of Matthew, Apostle and Evangelist: Psalm 34; Isaiah 33.13–17; Matthew 6.19–end
		Principal Service	**3rd Service**	**2nd Service**
Tuesday	**21 September** *R* Matthew, Apostle and Evangelist	Proverbs 3.13–18 Psalm 119.65–72 2 Corinthians 4.1–6 Matthew 9.9–13	*MP* Psalms 49, 117 1 Kings 19.15–end 2 Timothy 3.14–end	*EP* Psalm 119.33–40, 89–96 Ecclesiastes 5.4–12 Matthew 19.16–end
		Holy Communion	**Morning Prayer**	**Evening Prayer**
Wednesday	**22 September** *G* Ember Day	Proverbs 30.5–9 Psalm 119.105–112 Luke 9.1–6	Psalm **119.57–80** 1 Kings 17 Acts 20.1–16	Psalms **59**, 60 (67) Ecclesiasticus 2 *or* Ezekiel 2.3—3.11 Mark 13.1–13
Thursday	**23 September** *G*	Ecclesiastes 1.2–11 Psalm 90.1–6 Luke 9.7–9	Psalms 56, **57** (63*) 1 Kings 18.1–20 Acts 20.17–end	Psalms 61, **62**, 64 Ecclesiasticus 3.17–29 *or* Ezekiel 3.12–end Mark 13.14–23
Friday	**24 September** *G* Ember Day	Ecclesiastes 3.1–11 Psalm 144.1–4 Luke 9.18–22	Psalms **51**, 54 1 Kings 18.21–end Acts 21.1–16	Psalm **38** Ecclesiasticus 4.11–28 *or* Ezekiel 8 Mark.13.24–31
Saturday	**25 September** *Gw* Lancelot Andrewes, bishop, spiritual writer, 1626 (see p. 74) *Sergei of Radonezh, monastic reformer, teacher of the faith, 1392* Ember Day	Ecclesiastes 11.9—12.8 Psalm 90.1–2, 12–end Luke 9.43*b*–45	Psalm **68** 1 Kings 19 Acts 21.17–36	Psalms 65, **66** Ecclesiasticus 4.29—6.1 *or* Ezekiel 9 Mark 13.32–end

Trinity 17

		Principal Service	3rd Service	2nd Service
Sunday	**26 September** *G* **17th Sunday after Trinity** Proper 21	*Continuous:* Jeremiah 32.1–3*a*, 6–15 Psalm 91.1–6, 14–end [91.11–end] *Related:* Amos 6.1*a*, 4–7 Psalm 146 1 Timothy 6.6–19 Luke 16.19–end	Psalm 132 Isaiah 48.12–end Luke 11.37–end	Psalms 134, 135 [135.1–14] Nehemiah 2 John 8.31–38, 48–end

		Holy Communion	Morning Prayer	Evening Prayer
Monday	**27 September** *Gw* Vincent de Paul, founder of the Lazarists, 1660 (see p. 75) DEL week 26	Job 1.6–end Psalm 17.1–11 Luke 9.46–50	Psalm **71** 1 Kings 21 Acts 21.37—22.21	Psalms **72**, 75 Ecclesiasticus 6.14–end *or* Ezekiel 10.1–19 Mark 14.1–11
Tuesday	**28 September** *G*	Job 3.1–3, 11–17, 20–23 Psalm 88.14–19 Luke 9.51–56	Psalm **73** 1 Kings 22.1–28 Acts 22.22—23.11	Psalm **74** Ecclesiasticus 7.27–end *or* Ezekiel 11.14–end Mark 14.12–25 *or:* 1st EP of Michael and All Angels: Psalm 91; 2 Kings 6.8–17; Matthew 18.1–6, 10

		Principal Service	3rd Service	2nd Service
Wednesday	**29 September** *W* Michael and All Angels	Genesis 28.10–17 *or* Revelation 12.7–12 Psalm 103.19–end Revelation 12.7–12 *or* Hebrews 1.5–end John 1.47–end	*MP* Psalms 34, 150 Tobit 12.6–end *or* Daniel 12.1–4 Acts 12.1–11	*EP* Psalms 138, 148 Daniel 10.4–end Revelation 5

		Holy Communion	Morning Prayer	Evening Prayer
Thursday	**30 September** *G* *Jerome, translator, teacher of the faith, 420*	Job 19.21–27*a* Psalm 27.13–16 Luke 10.1–12	Psalm **78.1–39*** 2 Kings 1.2–17 Acts 24.1–23	Psalm **78.40–end*** Ecclesiasticus 11.7–28 *or* Ezekiel 12.17–end Mark 14.43–52
Friday	**1 October** *G* *Remigius, bishop, 533* *Anthony Ashley Cooper (Earl of Shaftesbury), social reformer, 1885*	Job 38.1, 12–21, 40.3–5 Psalm 139.6–11 Luke 10.13–16	Psalm **55** 2 Kings 2.1–18 Acts 24.24—25.12	Psalm **69** Ecclesiasticus 14.20—15.10 *or* Ezekiel 13.1–16 Mark 14.53–65
Saturday	**2 October** *G*	Job 42.1–3, 6, 12–end Psalm 119.169–end Luke 10.17–24	Psalms **76**, 79 2 Kings 4.1–37 Acts 25.13–end	Psalms 81, **84** Ecclesiasticus 15.11–end *or* Ezekiel 14.1–11 Mark 14.66–end

		Principal Service		3rd Service	2nd Service
Sunday	**3 October** *G* **18th Sunday after Trinity** Proper 22	*Continuous:* Lamentations 1.1–6 *Canticle:* Lamentations 3.19–26 *or* Psalm 137 [137.1–6] 2 Timothy 1.1–14 Luke 17.5–10	*Related:* Habakkuk 1.1–4; 2.1–4 Psalm 37.1–9	Psalm 141 Isaiah 49.13–23 Luke 12.1–12	Psalm 142 Nehemiah 5.1–13 John 9

		Holy Communion	Morning Prayer	Evening Prayer
Monday	**4 October** *Gw* Francis of Assisi, friar, deacon, 1226 (see p. 75) DEL week 27	Galatians 1.6–12 Psalm 111.1–6 Luke 10.25–37	Psalms **80**, 82 2 Kings 5 Acts 26.1–23	Psalms **85**, 86 Ecclesiasticus 16.17–end *or* Ezekiel 14.12–end Mark 15.1–15
Tuesday	**5 October** *G*	Galatians 1.13–end Psalm 139.1–9 Luke 10.38–end	Psalms 87, **89.1–18** 2 Kings 6.1–23 Acts 26.24–end	Psalm **89.19–end** Ecclesiasticus 17.1–24 *or* Ezekiel 18.1–20 Mark 15.16–32
Wednesday	**6 October** *Gr* William Tyndale, translator, martyr, 1536 (see p. 72)	Galatians 2.1–2, 7–14 Psalm 117 Luke 11.1–4	Psalm **119.105–128** 2 Kings 9.1–16 Acts 27.1–26	Psalms **91**, 93 Ecclesiasticus 18.1–14 *or* Ezekiel 18.21–32 Mark 15.33–41
Thursday	**7 October** *G*	Galatians 3.1–5 *Canticle:* Benedictus Luke 11.5–13	Psalms 90, **92** 2 Kings 9.17–end Acts 27.27–end	Psalm **94** Ecclesiasticus 19.4–17 *or* Ezekiel 20.1–20 Mark 15.42–end
Friday	**8 October** *G*	Galatians 3.7–14 Psalm 111.4–end Luke 11.15–26	Psalms **88** (95) 2 Kings 12.1–19 Acts 28.1–16	Psalm **102** Ecclesiasticus 19.20–end *or* Ezekiel 20.21–38 Mark 16.1–8
Saturday	**9 October** *G* *Denys, bishop, and companions, martyrs, c.250* *Robert Grosseteste, bishop, philosopher, scientist, 1253*	Galatians 3.22–end Psalm 105.1–7 Luke 11.27–28	Psalms 96, **97**, 100 2 Kings 17.1–23 Acts 28.17–end	Psalm **104** Ecclesiasticus 21.1–17 *or* Ezekiel 24.15–end Mark 16.9–end

		Principal Service	3rd Service	2nd Service
Sunday	**10 October** *G* **19th Sunday after Trinity** Proper 23	*Continuous:* Jeremiah 29.1, 4–7 Psalm 66.1–11 *Related:* 2 Kings 5.1–3, 7–15c Psalm 111 2 Timothy 2.8–15 Luke 17.11–19	Psalm 143 Isaiah 50.4–10 Luke 13.22–30	Psalm 144 Nehemiah 6.1–16 John 15.12–end
		Holy Communion	**Morning Prayer**	**Evening Prayer**
Monday	**11 October** *G* *Ethelburga, abbess, 675* *James the Deacon,* *companion of Paulinus, 7th cent.* DEL week 28	Galatians 4.21–24, 26–27, 31, 5.1 Psalm 113 Luke 11.29–32	Psalms **98**, 99, 101 2 Kings 17.24–end Philippians 1.1–11	Psalms **105*** (*or* 103) Ecclesiasticus 22.6–22 *or* Ezekiel 28.1–19 John 13.1–11
Tuesday	**12 October** *Gw* Wilfrid, bishop, missionary, 709 (see p. 75) *Elizabeth Fry, prison reformer, 1845* *Edith Cavell, nurse, 1915*	Galatians 5.1–6 Psalm 119.41–48 Luke 11.37–41	Psalms **106*** (*or* 103) 2 Kings 18.1–12 Philippians 1.12–end	Psalm **107*** Ecclesiasticus 22.27—23.15 *or* Ezekiel 33.1–20 John 13.12–20
Wednesday	**13 October** *Gw* Edward the Confessor, king, 1066 (see p. 76)	Galatians 5.18–end Psalm 1 Luke 11.42–46	Psalms 110, **111**, 112 2 Kings 18.13–end Philippians 2.1–13	Psalm **119.129–152** Ecclesiasticus 24.1–22 *or* Ezekiel 33.21–end John 13.21–30
Thursday	**14 October** *G*	Ephesians 1.1–10 Psalm 98.1–4 Luke 11.47–end	Psalms 113, **115** 2 Kings 19.1–19 Philippians 2.14–end	Psalms 114, **116**, 117 Ecclesiasticus 24.23–end *or* Ezekiel 34.1–16 John 13.31–end
Friday	**15 October** *Gw* Teresa of Avila, teacher of the faith, 1582 (see p. 73)	Ephesians 1.11–14 Psalm 33.1–6, 12 Luke 12.1–7	Psalm **139** 2 Kings 19.20–36 Philippians 3.1—4.1	Psalms **130**, 131, 137 Ecclesiasticus 27.30—28.9 *or* Ezekiel 34.17–end John 14.1–14
Saturday	**16 October** *G* *Nicholas Ridley and Hugh Latimer,* *bishops, martyrs, 1555*	Ephesians 1.15–end Psalm **8** Luke 12.8–12	Psalms 120, **121**, 122 2 Kings 20 Philippians 4.2–end	Psalm **118** Ecclesiasticus 28.14–end *or* Ezekiel 36.16–36 John 14.15–end

			Principal Service	3rd Service	2nd Service
Sunday	**17 October** **20th Sunday after Trinity** Proper 24	*G*	*Continuous:* Jeremiah 31.27–34 Psalm 119.97–104 *Related:* Genesis 32.22–31 Psalm 121 2 Timothy 3.14—4.5 Luke 18.1–8	Psalm 147 Isaiah 54.1–14 Luke 13.31–end	Psalms [146] 149 Nehemiah 8.9–end John 16.1–11 *or:* 1st EP of Luke the Evangelist: Psalm 33; Hosea 6.1–3; 2 Timothy 3.10–end
Monday	**18 October** Luke the Evangelist	R	Isaiah 35.3–6 *or* Acts 16.6–12*a* Psalm 147.1–7 2 Timothy 4.5–17 Luke 10.1–9	*MP* Psalms 145, 146 Isaiah 55 Luke 1.1–4 Colossians 4.7–end	*EP* Psalm 103 Ecclesiasticus 38.1–14 *or* Isaiah 61.1–6
			Holy Communion	**Morning Prayer**	**Evening Prayer**
Tuesday	**19 October** Henry Martyn, translator, missionary, 1812 (see p. 75) DEL week 29	*Gw*	Ephesians 2.12–end Psalm 85.7–end Luke 12.35–38	Psalms **132**, 133 2 Kings 22.1—23.3 1 Timothy 1.18—end of 2	Psalms (134,) **135** Ecclesiasticus 34.9–end *or* Ezekiel 37.15–end John 15.12–17
Wednesday	**20 October**	*G*	Ephesians 3.2–12 Psalm 98 Luke 12.39–48	Psalm **119.153–end** 2 Kings 23.4–25 1 Timothy 3	Psalm **136** Ecclesiasticus 35 *or* Ezekiel 39.21–end John 15.18–end
Thursday	**21 October**	*G*	Ephesians 3.14–end Psalm 33.1–6 Luke 12.49–53	Psalms **143**, 146 2 Kings 23.36—24.17 1 Timothy 4	Psalms **138**, 140, 141 Ecclesiasticus 37.7–24 *or* Ezekiel 43.1–12 John 16.1–15
Friday	**22 October**	*G*	Ephesians 4.1–6 Psalm 24.1–6 Luke 12.54–end	Psalms 142, **144** 2 Kings 24.18—25.12 1 Timothy 5.1–16	Psalm **145** Ecclesiasticus 38.1–14 *or* Ezekiel 44.4–16 John 16.16–22
Saturday	**23 October**	*G*	Ephesians 4.7–16 Psalm 122 Luke 13.1–9	Psalm **147** 2 Kings 25.22–end 1 Timothy 5.17–end	Psalms **148**, 149, 150 Ecclesiasticus 38.24–end *or* Ezekiel 47.1–12 John 16.23–end

		Principal Service	3rd Service	2nd Service
Sunday	**24 October** *G* **Last Sunday after Trinity** Proper 25	*Continuous:* Joel 2.23–end Psalm 65 [65.1–7] *Related:* Ecclesiasticus 35.12–17 *or* Jeremiah 14.7–10, 19–end Psalm 84.1–7 2 Timothy 4.6–8, 16–18 Luke 18.9–14	Psalm 119.105–128 Isaiah 59.9–20 Luke 14.1–14	Psalm 119.1–16 Ecclesiastes 11, 12 2 Timothy 2.1–7 *HC* Matthew 22.34–end

or, when the date of dedication of a church is not known, the Dedication Festival *(W) may be celebrated today or on 3 October, or on a suitable date chosen locally (see p. 71).*
If the Last Sunday after Trinity is being observed as **Bible Sunday**:

		Principal Service	3rd Service	2nd Service
or **Sunday**	**24 October** *G* **Bible Sunday**	Isaiah 45.22–end Psalm 119.129–136 Romans 15.1–6 Luke 4.16–24	Psalm 119.105–128 1 Kings 22.1–17 Romans 15.4–13 *or* Luke 14.1–14	Psalm 119.1–16 Jeremiah 36.9–end Romans 10.5–17 *HC* Matthew 22.34–40

		Holy Communion	Morning Prayer	Evening Prayer
Monday	**25 October** *G* *Crispin and Crispinian, martyrs, c.287* DEL week 30	Ephesians 4.32—5.8 Psalm 1 Luke 13.10–17	Psalms **1**, 2, 3 Judith 4 *or* Exodus 22.21–27, 23.1–17 1 Timothy 6.1–10	Psalms **4**, 7 Ecclesiasticus 39.1–11 *or* Ecclesiastes 1 John 17.1–5
Tuesday	**26 October** *Gw* Alfred, king, scholar, 899 (see p. 76) *Cedd, abbot, bishop, 664*	Ephesians 5.21–end Psalm 128 Luke 13.18–21	Psalms **5**, 6 (8) Judith 5.1—6.4 *or* Exodus 29.38—30.16 1 Timothy 6.11–end	Psalms **9**, 10* Ecclesiasticus 39.13–end *or* Ecclesiastes 2 John 17.6–19
Wednesday	**27 October** *G*	Ephesians 6.1–9 Psalm 145.10–20 Luke 13.22–30	Psalm **119.1–32** Judith 6.10—7.7 *or* Leviticus 8 2 Timothy 1.1–14	Psalms **11**, 12, 13 Ecclesiasticus 42.15–end *or* Ecclesiastes 3.1–15 John 17.20–end *or:* 1st EP of Simon and Jude, Apostles: Psalms 124, 125, 126; Deuteronomy 32.1–4; John 14.15–26

		Principal Service	3rd Service	2nd Service
Thursday	**28 October** *R* Simon and Jude, Apostles	Isaiah 28.14–16 Psalm 119.89–96 Ephesians 2.19–end John 15.17–end	*MP* Psalms 116, 117 Wisdom 5.1–16 *or* Isaiah 45.18–end Luke 6.12–16	*EP* Psalm 119.1–16 1 Maccabees 2.42–66 *or* Jeremiah 3.11–18 Jude vv1–4, 17–end
		Holy Communion	**Morning Prayer**	**Evening Prayer**
Friday	**29 October** *Gr* James Hannington, bishop, martyr, 1885 (see p. 72)	Philippians 1.1–11 Psalm 111 Luke 14.1–6	Psalms 17, **19** Judith 8.9–end *or* Leviticus 16.2–24 2 Timothy 2.14–end	Psalm **22** Ecclesiasticus 43.13–end *or* Ecclesiastes 5 John 18.12–27
Saturday	**30 October** *G*	Philippians 1.18–26 Psalm 42.1–7 Luke 14.1, 7–11	Psalms 20, 21, **23** Judith 9 *or* Leviticus 17 2 Timothy 3	Psalms **24**, 25 Ecclesiasticus 44.1–15 *or* Ecclesiastes 6 John 18.28–end *or, if All Saints' Day is celebrated on Sunday 31 October only:* **1st EP of All Saints' Day:** Psalms 1, 5; Ecclesiasticus 44.1–15 *or* Isaiah 40.27–end; Revelation 19.6–10

4 before Advent / All Saints' Day

All Saints' Day is celebrated on either Monday 1 November or Sunday 31 October; if the latter, there may be a supplementary celebration on 1 November.

Where All Saints' Day is celebrated on Monday 1 November only:

			Principal Service	3rd Service	2nd Service
Sunday	**31 October** **4th Sunday before Advent**	*R/G*	Isaiah 1.10–18 Psalm 32.1–8 2 Thessalonians 1 Luke 19.1–10	Psalm 87 Job 26 Colossians 1.9–14	Psalm 145 [*or* 145.1–9] Lamentations 3.22–33 John 11.[1–31] 32–44 *or:* **1st EP of All Saints' Day:** Psalms 1, 5; Ecclesiasticus 44.1–15 *or* Isaiah 40.27–end; Revelation 19.6–10
Monday	**1 November** **All Saints' Day**	*Gold or W*	Daniel 7.1–3, 15–18 Psalm 149 Ephesians 1.11–end	*MP* Psalms 15, 84, 149 Isaiah 35 Luke 9.18–27	*EP* Psalms 148, 150 Isaiah 65.17–end Hebrews 11.32—12.2

Where All Saints' Day is celebrated on Sunday 31 October only:

			Principal Service	3rd Service	2nd Service
Sunday	**31 October** **All Saints' Day**	*Gold or W*	Daniel 7.1–3, 15–18 Psalm 149 Ephesians 1.11–end Luke 6.20–31	*MP* Psalms 15, 84, 149 Isaiah 35 Luke 9.18–27	*EP* Psalms 148, 150 Isaiah 65.17–end Hebrews 11.32—12.2
			Holy Communion	**Morning Prayer**	**Evening Prayer**
Monday	**1 November** DEL week 31	*R/G*	Philippians 2.1–4 Psalm 131 Luke 14.12–14	Psalms **2**, 146 *or* 27, **30** Daniel 1 Revelation 1	Psalms **92**, 96, 97 *or* 26, **28**, 29 Isaiah 1.1–20 Matthew 1.18–end

Where All Saints' Day is celebrated on Monday 1 November in addition to Sunday 31 October:

			Principal Service	3rd Service	2nd Service
Monday	**1 November** **All Saints' Day**	*Gold or W*	Isaiah 56.3–8 *or* 2 Esdras 2.42–end Psalm 33.1–5 Hebrews 12.18–24 Matthew 5.1–12	*MP* Psalms 111, 112, 117 Wisdom 5.1–16 *or* Jeremiah 31.31–34 2 Corinthians 4.5–12	*EP* Psalm 145 Isaiah 66.20–23 Colossians 1.9–14

			Holy Communion	Morning Prayer	Evening Prayer
Tuesday	**2 November** Commemoration of the Faithful Departed (All Souls' Day)	*Rp/Gp*	Philippians 2.5–11 Psalm 22.22–27 Luke 14.15–24 *Lesser Festival eucharistic lectionary:* Lamentations 3.17–26, 31–33 *or* Wisdom 3.1–9; Psalm 23 *or* 27.1–6, 16–end Romans 5.5–11 *or* 1 Peter 1.3–9 John 5.19–25 *or* John 6.37–40	Psalms **5**, 147.1–12 *or* 32, **36** Daniel 2.1–24 Revelation 2.1–11	Psalms 98, 99, **100** *or* **33** Isaiah 1.21–end Matthew 2.1–15
Wednesday	**3 November** Richard Hooker, priest, teacher of the faith, 1600 (see p. 73) *Martin of Porres, friar, 1639*	*Rw/Gw*	Philippians 2.12–18 Psalm 27.1–5 Luke 14.25–33	Psalms **9**, 147.13–end *or* **34** Daniel 2.25–end Revelation 2.12–end	Psalms 111, **112**, 116 *or* **119.33–56** Isaiah 2.1–11 Matthew 2.16–end
Thursday	**4 November**	*R/G*	Philippians 3.3–8*a* Psalm 105.1–7 Luke 15.1–10	Psalms 11, **15**, 148 *or* **37*** Daniel 3.1–18 Revelation 3.1–13	Psalms **118** *or* 39, **40** Isaiah 2.12–end Matthew 3
Friday	**5 November**	*R/G*	Philippians 3.17—4.1 Psalm 122 Luke 16.1–8	Psalms **16**, 149 *or* **31** Daniel 3.19–end Revelation 3.14–end	Psalms 137, 138, **143** *or* **35** Isaiah 3.1–15 Matthew 4.1–11
Saturday	**6 November** *Leonard, hermit, 6th cent.* *William Temple, archbishop, teacher of the faith, 1944*	*R/G*	Philippians 4.10–19 Psalm 112 Luke 16.9–15	Psalms **18.31–end**, 150 *or* 41, **42**, 43 Daniel 4.1–18 Revelation 4	Psalms **145** *or* 45, **46** Isaiah 4.2—5.7 Matthew 4.12–22

3 before Advent

		Principal Service	3rd Service	2nd Service
Sunday	**7 November** *R/G* **3rd Sunday before Advent**	Job 19.23–27*a* Psalm 17.1–9 [17.1–8] 2 Thessalonians 2.1–5, 13–end Luke 20.27–38	Psalms 20, 90 Isaiah 2.1–5 James 3.13–end	Psalm 40 1 Kings 3.1–15 Romans 8.31–end *HC* Matthew 22.15–22
		Holy Communion	**Morning Prayer**	**Evening Prayer**
Monday	**8 November** *Rw/Gw* Saints and martyrs of England DEL week 32	Titus 1.1–9 Psalm 24.1–6 Luke 17.1–6 *Lesser Festival eucharistic lectionary:* Isaiah 61.4–9 *or* Ecclesiasticus 44.1–15; Psalm 15; Revelation 19.5–10; John 17.18–23	Psalms 19, **20** *or* **44** Daniel 4.19–end Revelation 5	Psalms **34** *or* **47**, 49 Isaiah 5.8–24 Matthew 4.23—5.12
Tuesday	**9 November** *R/G* *Margery Kempe, mystic, c.1440*	Titus 2.1–8, 11–14 Psalm 37.3–5, 30–32 Luke 17.7–10	Psalms **21**, 24 *or* **48**, 52 Daniel 5.1–12 Revelation 6	Psalms 36, **40** *or* **50** Isaiah 5.25–end Matthew 5.13–20
Wednesday	**10 November** *Rw/Gw* Leo the Great, bishop, teacher of the faith, 461 (see p. 73)	Titus 3.1–7 Psalm 23 Luke 17.11–19	Psalms **23**, 25 *or* **119.57–80** Daniel 5.13–end Revelation 7.1–4, 9–end	Psalms **37** *or* **59**, 60 (67) Isaiah 6 Matthew 5.21–37
Thursday	**11 November** *Rw/Gw* Martin, bishop, c.397 (see p. 74)	Philemon 7–20 Psalm 146.4–end Luke 17.20–25	Psalms **26**, 27 *or* 56, **57** (63*) Daniel 6 Revelation 8	Psalms 42, **43** *or* 61, **62**, 64 Isaiah 7.1–17 Matthew 5.38–end
Friday	**12 November** *R/G*	2 John 4–9 Psalm 119.1–8 Luke 17.26–end	Psalms 28, **32** *or* **51**, 54 Daniel 7.1–14 Revelation 9.1–12	Psalm **31** *or* **38** Isaiah 8.1–15 Matthew 6.1–18
Saturday	**13 November** *Rw/Gw* Charles Simeon, priest, evangelical divine, 1836 (see p. 74)	3 John 5–8 Psalm 112 Luke 18.1–8	Psalm **33** *or* **68** Daniel 7.15–end Revelation 9.13–end	Psalms 84, **86** *or* 65, **66** Isaiah 8.16—9.7 Matthew 6.19–end

		Principal Service	3rd Service	2nd Service
Sunday	**14 November** *R/G* **2nd Sunday before Advent** *Remembrance Sunday*	Malachi 4.1–2*a* Psalm 98 2 Thessalonians 3.6–13 Luke 21.5–19	Psalm 132 1 Samuel 16.1–13 Matthew 13.44–52	Psalm [93] 97 Daniel 6 Matthew 13.1–9, 18–23
		Holy Communion	**Morning Prayer**	**Evening Prayer**
Monday	**15 November** *R/G* DEL week 33	Revelation 1.1–4; 2.1–5 Psalm 1 Luke 18.35–end	Psalms 46, **47** *or* **71** Daniel 8.1–14 Revelation 10	Psalms 70, **71** *or* **72**, 75 Isaiah 9.8—10.4 Matthew 7.1–12
Tuesday	**16 November** *Rw/Gw* Margaret, queen, philanthropist, 1093 (see p. 76) *Edmund Rich, archbishop, 1240*	Revelation 3.1–6; 14–end Psalm 15 Luke 19.1–10	Psalms 48, **52** *or* **73** Daniel 8.15–end Revelation 11.1–14	Psalms **67**, 72 *or* **74** Isaiah 10.5–19 Matthew 7.13–end
Wednesday	**17 November** *Rw/Gw* Hugh, bishop, 1200 (see p. 74)	Revelation 4 Psalm 150 Luke 19.11–28	Psalms **56**, 57 *or* **77** Daniel 9.1–19 Revelation 11.15–end	Psalm **73** *or* **119.81–104** Isaiah 10.20–32 Matthew 8.1–13
Thursday	**18 November** *Rw/Gw* Elizabeth, princess, philanthropist, 1231 (see p. 76)	Revelation 5.1–10 Psalm 149.1–5 Luke 19.41–44	Psalms 61, **62** *or* **78.1–39*** Daniel 9.20–end Revelation 12	Psalms 74, **76** *or* **78.40–end*** Isaiah 10.33—11.9 Matthew 8.14–22
Friday	**19 November** *Rw/Gw* Hilda, abbess, 680 (see p. 75) *Mechtild, béguine, mystic, 1280*	Revelation 10.8–end Psalm 119.65–72 Luke 19.45–end	Psalms **63**, 65 *or* **55** Daniel 10.1—11.1 Revelation 13.1–10	Psalm **77** *or* **69** Isaiah 11.10—end of 12 Matthew 8.23–end
Saturday	**20 November** *R/Gr* Edmund, king, martyr, 870 (see p. 72) *Priscilla Lydia Sellon, a restorer of the religious life in the Church of England, 1876*	Revelation 11.4–12 Psalm 144.1–9 Luke 20.27–40	Psalms **78.1–39** *or* **76**, 79 Daniel 12 Revelation 13.11–end	Psalms **78.40–end** *or* 81, **84** Isaiah 13.1–13 Matthew 9.1–17 *or:* 1st EP of Christ the King: Psalms 99, 100; Isaiah 10.33—11.9; 1 Timothy 6.11–16

Christ the King / Sunday next before Advent

			Principal Service	3rd Service	2nd Service
Sunday	**21 November** Christ the King *Sunday next before Advent*	*R/W*	Jeremiah 23.1–6 Psalm 46 Colossians 1.11–20 Luke 23.33–43	*MP* Psalms 29, 110 Zechariah 6.9–end Revelation 11.15–18	*EP* Psalm 72 [72.1–7] 1 Samuel 8.4–20 John 18.33–37
			Holy Communion	**Morning Prayer**	**Evening Prayer**
Monday	**22 November** *Cecilia, martyr, c.230* DEL week 34	*R/G*	Revelation 14.1–5 Psalm 24.1–6 Luke 21.1–4	Psalms 92, **96** *or* **80**, 82 Isaiah 40.1–11 Revelation 14.1–13	Psalms **80**, 81 *or* **85**, 86 Isaiah 14.3–20 Matthew 9.18–34
Tuesday	**23 November** Clement, bishop, martyr, *c.*100 (see p. 72)	*R/Gr*	Revelation 14.14–19 Psalm 96 Luke 21.5–11	Psalms **97**, 98, 100 *or* 87, **89.1–18** Isaiah 40.12–26 Revelation 14.14—end of 15	Psalms 99, **101** *or* **89.19–end** Isaiah 17 Matthew 9.35—10.15
Wednesday	**24 November**	*R/G*	Revelation 15.1–4 Psalm 98 Luke 21.12–19	Psalms 110, 111, **112** *or* **119.105–128** Isaiah 40.27—41.7 Revelation 16.1–11	Psalms 121, **122**, 123, 124 *or* **91**, 93 Isaiah 19 Matthew 10.16–33
Thursday	**25 November** *Catherine, martyr, 4th cent.* *Isaac Watts, hymn writer, 1748*	*R/G*	Revelation 18.1–2, 21–23; 19.1–3, 9 Psalm 100 Luke 21.20–28	Psalms **125**, 126, 127, 128 *or* 90, **92** Isaiah 41.8–20 Revelation 16.12–end	Psalms 131, 132, **133** *or* **94** Isaiah 21.1–12 Matthew 10.34—11.1
Friday	**26 November**	*R/G*	Revelation 20.1–4, 11—21.2 Psalm 84.1–6 Luke 21.29–33	Psalms **139** *or* **88** (95) Isaiah 41.21—42.9 Revelation 17	Psalms **146**, 147 *or* **102** Isaiah 22.1–14 Matthew 11.2–19
Saturday	**27 November**	*R/G*	Revelation 22.1–7 Psalm 95.1–7 Luke 21.34–36	Psalms **145** *or* 96, **97**, 100 Isaiah 42.10–17 Revelation 18	Psalms 148, 149, **150** *or* **104** Isaiah 24 Matthew 11.20–end

¶ *Collects and Post Communions*

All the contemporary language Collects and Post Communions, including the Additional Collects, may be found in *Common Worship: Collects and Post Communions* (Church House Publishing: London, 2004). The Additional Collects are also published separately.

The contemporary language Collects and Post Communions, apart from the Additional Collects, appear in the other Common Worship volumes as follows:

¶ President's edition: all Collects and Post Communions;
¶ *Daily Prayer*: all Collects;
¶ main volume: Collects and Post Communions for Sundays, Principal Feasts and Holy Days, and Festivals;
¶ *Festivals*: Collects and Post Communions for Festivals, Lesser Festivals, Common of the Saints and Special Occasions.

The traditional-language Collects and Post Communions all appear in the president's edition. They appear in other publications as follows:

¶ main volume: Collects and Post Communions for Sundays, Principal Feasts and Holy Days, and Festivals;
¶ separate booklet: Collects and Post Communions for Lesser Festivals, Common of the Saints and Special Occasions.

¶ *Lectionary for Dedication Festival*

If date not known, observe on the first Sunday in October or Last Sunday after Trinity.

Evening Prayer on the Eve
Psalm 24
2 Chronicles 7.11–16
John 4.19–29

Dedication Festival
Gold or White

	Principal Service	3rd Service	2nd Service	Psalmody
Year A	1 Kings 8.22–30 *or* Revelation 21.9–14 Psalm 122 Hebrews 12.18–24 Matthew 21.12–16	Haggai 2.6–9 Hebrews 10.19–25	Jeremiah 7.1–11 1 Corinthians 3.9–17 *HC* Luke 19.1–10	*MP* 48, 150 *EP* 132
Year B	Genesis 28.11–18 *or* Revelation 21.9–14 Psalm 122 1 Peter 2.1–10 John 10.22–29	Haggai 2.6–9 Hebrews 10.19–25	Jeremiah 7.1–11 Luke 19.1–10	*MP* 48, 150 *EP* 132
Year C	1 Chronicles 29.6–19 Psalm 122 Ephesians 2.19–22 John 2.13–22	Haggai 2.6–9 Hebrews 10.19–25	Jeremiah 7.1–11 Luke 19.1–10	*MP* 48, 150 *EP* 132

¶ *Lectionary for Common of the Saints*

The Blessed Virgin Mary

Genesis 3.8–15, 20; Isaiah 7.10–14; Micah 5.1–4
Psalms 45.10–17; 113; 131
Acts 1.12–14; Romans 8.18–30; Galatians 4.4–7
Luke 1.26–38; *or* 1.39–47; John 19.25–27

Martyrs

2 Chronicles 24.17–21; Isaiah 43.1–7; Jeremiah 11.18–20; Wisdom 4.10–15
Psalms 3; 11; 31.1–5; 44.18–24; 126
Romans 8.35–end; 2 Corinthians 4.7–15; 2 Timothy 2.3–7 [8–13]; Hebrews 11.32–end; 1 Peter 4.12–end; Revelation 12.10–12*a*
Matthew 10.16–22; *or* 10.28–39; *or* 16.24–26; John 12.24–26; *or* 15.18–21

Agnes (21 Jan): *also* Revelation 7.13–end
Alban (22 June): *especially* 2 Timothy 2.3–13; John 12.24–26
Alphege (19 Apr): *also* Hebrews 5.1–4
Boniface (5 June): *also* Acts 20.24–28
Charles (30 Jan): *also* Ecclesiasticus 2.12–end; 1 Timothy 6.12–16
Clement (23 Nov): *also* Philippians 3.17—4.3; Matthew 16.13–19
Cyprian (15 Sept): *especially* 1 Peter 4.12–end; *also* Matthew 18.18–22
Edmund (20 Nov): *also* Proverbs 20.28; 21.1–4, 7
Ignatius (17 Oct): *also* Philippians 3.7–12; John 6.52–58
James Hannington (29 Oct): *especially* Matthew 10.28–39
Janani Luwum (17 Feb): *also* Ecclesiasticus 4.20–28; John 12.24–32
John Coleridge Patteson (20 Sept): *especially* 2 Chronicles 24.17–21; *also* Acts 7.55–end
Justin (1 June): *especially* John 15.18–21; *also* 1 Maccabees 2.15–22; 1 Corinthians 1.18–25
Laurence (10 Aug): *also* 2 Corinthians 9.6–10
Lucy (13 Dec): *also* Wisdom 3.1–7; 2 Corinthians 4.6–15
Oswald (5 Aug): *especially* 1 Peter 4.12–end; John 16.29–end
Perpetua, Felicity and comps (7 Mar): *especially* Revelation 12.10–12*a*; *also* Wisdom 3.1–7
Polycarp (23 Feb): *also* Revelation 2.8–11
Thomas Becket (29 Dec *or* 7 Jul): *especially* Matthew 10.28–33; *also* Ecclesiasticus 51.1–8
William Tyndale (6 Oct): *also* Proverbs 8.4–11; 2 Timothy 3.12–end

Teachers of the Faith and Spiritual Writers

1 Kings 3.[6–10] 11–14; Proverbs 4.1–9; Wisdom 7.7–10, 15–16; Ecclesiasticus 39.1–10
Psalms 19.7–10; 34.11–17; 37.31–35; 119.89–96; 119.97–104
1 Corinthians 1.18–25; *or* 2.1–10; *or* 2.9–end; Ephesians 3.8–12; 2 Timothy 4.1–8; Titus 2.1–8
Matthew 5.13–19; *or* 13.52–end; *or* 23.8–12; Mark 4.1–9; John 16.12–15

Ambrose (7 Dec): *also* Isaiah 41.9*b*–13; Luke 22.24–30
Anselm (21 Apr): *also* Wisdom 9.13–end; Romans 5.8–11
Athanasius (2 May): *also* Ecclesiasticus 4.20–28; *also* Matthew 10.24–27
Augustine of Hippo (28 Aug): *especially* Ecclesiasticus 39.1–10; *also* Romans 13.11–13
Basil and Gregory (2 Jan): *especially* 2 Timothy 4.1–8; Matthew 5.13–19
Bernard (20 Aug): *especially* Revelation 19.5–9
Catherine of Siena (29 Apr): *also* Proverbs 8.1, 6–11; John 17.12–end
Francis de Sales (24 Jan): *also* Proverbs 3.13–18; John 3.17–21
Gregory the Great (3 Sept): *also* 1 Thessalonians 2.3–8
Gregory of Nyssa and Macrina (19 July): *especially* 1 Corinthians 2.9–13; *also* Wisdom 9.13–17
Hilary (13 Jan): *also* 1 John 2.18–25; John 8.25–32
Irenaeus (28 June): *also* 2 Peter 1.16–end
Jeremy Taylor (13 Aug): *also* Titus 2.7–8, 11–14
John Bunyan (30 Aug): *also* Hebrews 12.1–2; Luke 21.21, 34–36
John Chrysostom (13 Sept): *especially* Matthew 5.13–19; *also* Jeremiah 1.4–10
John of the Cross (14 Dec): *especially* 1 Corinthians 2.1–10; *also* John 14.18–23
Leo (10 Nov): *also* 1 Peter 5.1–11
Richard Hooker (3 Nov): *especially* John 16.12–15; *also* Ecclesiasticus 44.10–15
Teresa of Avila (15 Oct): *also* Romans 8.22–27
Thomas Aquinas (28 Jan): *especially* Wisdom 7.7–10, 15–16; 1 Corinthians 2.9–end; John 16.12–15
William Law (10 Apr): *especially* 1 Corinthians 2.9–end; *also* Matthew 17.1–9

Bishops and Other Pastors

1 Samuel 16.1, 6–13; Isaiah 6.1–8; Jeremiah 1.4–10; Ezekiel 3.16–21; Malachi 2.5–7
Psalms 1; 15; 16.5–end; 96; 110
Acts 20.28–35; 1 Corinthians 4.1–5; 2 Corinthians 4.1–10 [*or* 1–2, 5–7];
or 5.14–20; 1 Peter 5.1–4
Matthew 11.25–end; *or* 24.42–46; John 10.11–16; *or* 15.9–17; *or* 21.15–17

Augustine of Canterbury (26 May): *also* 1 Thessalonians 2.2*b*–8; Matthew 13.31–33
Charles Simeon (13 Nov): *especially* Malachi 2.5–7; *also* Colossians 1.3–8; Luke 8.4–8
David (1 Mar): *also* 2 Samuel 23.1–4; Psalm 89.19–22, 24
Dunstan (19 May): *especially* Matthew 24.42–46; *also* Exodus 31.1–5
Edward King (8 Mar): *also* Hebrews 13.1–8
George Herbert (27 Feb): *especially* Malachi 2.5–7; Matthew 11.25–end;
also Revelation 19.5–9
Hugh (17 Nov): *also* 1 Timothy 6.11–16
John Keble (14 July): *also* Lamentations 3.19–26; Matthew 5.1–8
John and Charles Wesley (24 May): *also* Ephesians 5.15–20
Lancelot Andrewes (25 Sept): *especially* Isaiah 6.1–8
Martin of Tours (11 Nov): *also* 1 Thessalonians 5.1–11; Matthew 25.34–40
Nicholas (6 Dec): *also* Isaiah 61.1–3; 1 Timothy 6.6–11; Mark 10.13–16
Richard (16 June): *also* John 21.15–19
Swithun (15 July): *also* James 5.7–11, 13–18
Thomas Ken (8 June): *especially* 2 Corinthians 4.1–10 [*or* 1–2, 5–7]; Matthew 24.42–46
Wulfstan (19 Jan): *especially* Matthew 24.42–46

Members of Religious Communities

1 Kings 19.9–18; Proverbs 10.27–end; Song of Solomon 8.6–7; Isaiah 61.10—62.5; Hosea 2.14–15, 19–20

Psalms 34.1–8; 112.1–9; 119.57–64; 123; 131

Acts 4.32–35; 2 Corinthians 10.17—11.2; Philippians 3.7–14; 1 John 2.15–17; Revelation 19.1, 5–9

Matthew 11.25–end; *or* 19.3–12; *or* 19.23–end; Luke 9.57–end; *or* 12.32–37

Aelred (12 Jan): *also* Ecclesiasticus 15.1–6
Alcuin (20 May): *also* Colossians 3.12–16; John 4.19–24
Antony (17 Jan): *especially* Philippians 3.7–14, *also* Matthew 19.16–26
Bede (25 May): *also* Ecclesiasticus 39.1–10
Benedict (11 July): *also* 1 Corinthians 3.10–11; Luke 18.18–22
Clare (11 Aug): *especially* Song of Solomon 8.6–7
Dominic (8 Aug): *also* Ecclesiasticus 39.1–10
Etheldreda (23 June): *also* Matthew 25.1–13
Francis of Assisi (4 Oct): *also* Galatians 6.14–end; Luke 12.22–34
Hilda (19 Nov): *especially* Isaiah 61.10—62.5
Hildegard (17 Sept): *also* 1 Corinthians 2.9–13; Luke 10.21–24
Julian of Norwich (8 May): *also* 1 Corinthians 13.8–end; Matthew 5.13–16
Vincent de Paul (27 Sept): *also* 1 Corinthians 1.25–end; Matthew 25.34–40

Missionaries

Isaiah 52.7–10; *or* 61.1–3*a*; Ezekiel 34.11–16; Jonah 3.1–5

Psalms 67; *or* 87; *or* 97; *or* 100; *or* 117

Acts 2.14, 22–36; *or* 13.46–49; *or* 16.6–10; *or* 26.19–23; Romans 15.17–21; 2 Corinthians 5.11—6.2

Matthew 9.35–end; *or* 28.16–end; Mark 16.15–20; Luke 5.1–11; *or* 10.1–9

Aidan (31 Aug): *also* 1 Corinthians 9.16–19
Anskar (3 Feb): *especially* Isaiah 52.7–10; *also* Romans 10.11–15
Chad (2 Mar *or* 26 Oct): *also* 1 Timothy 6.11*b*–16
Columba (9 June): *also* Titus 2.11–end
Cuthbert (20 Mar *or* 4 Sept): *especially* Ezekiel 34.11–16; *also* Matthew 18.12–14
Cyril and Methodius (14 Feb): *especially* Isaiah 52.7–10; *also* Romans 10.11–15
Henry Martyn (19 Oct): *especially* Mark 16.15–end; *also* Isaiah 55.6–11
Ninian (16 Sept): *especially* Acts 13.46–49; Mark 16.15–end
Patrick (17 Mar): *also* Psalm 91.1–4, 13–16; Luke 10.1–12, 17–20
Paulinus (10 Oct): *especially* Matthew 28.16–end
Wilfrid (12 Oct): *especially* Luke 5.1–11; *also* 1 Corinthians 1.18–25
Willibrord (7 Nov): *especially* Isaiah 52.7–10; Matthew 28.16–end

Any Saint

General

Genesis 12.1–4; Proverbs 8.1–11; Micah 6.6–8; Ecclesiasticus 2.7–13 [14–end]
Psalms 32; 33.1–5; 119.1–8; 139.1–4 [5–12]; 145.8–14
Ephesians 3.14–19; *or* 6.11–18; Hebrews 13.7–8, 15–16; James 2.14–17;
I John 4.7–16; Revelation 21.[1–4] 5–7
Matthew 19.16–21; *or* 25.1–13; *or* 25.14–30; John 15.1–8; *or* 17.20–end

Christian rulers

I Samuel 16.1–13*a*; I Kings 3.3–14
Psalms 72.1–7; 99
I Timothy 2.1–6
Mark 10.42–45; Luke 14.27–33

Alfred the Great (26 Oct): *also* 2 Samuel 23.1–5; John 18.33–37
Edward the Confessor (13 Oct): *also* 2 Samuel 23.1–5; I John 4.13–16
Margaret of Scotland (16 Nov): *also* Proverbs 31.10–12, 20, 26–end;
I Corinthians 12.13—13.3; Matthew 25.34–end

Those working for the poor and underprivileged

Isaiah 58.6–11
Psalms 82; 146.5–10
Hebrews 13.1–3; I John 3.14–18
Matthew 5.1–12; *or* 25.31–end

Elizabeth of Hungary (18 Nov): *especially* Matthew 25.31–end; *also* Proverbs 31.10–end
Josephine Butler (30 May): *especially* Isaiah 58.6–11; *also* I John 3.18–23; Matthew 9.10–13
William Wilberforce (30 July): *also* Job 31.16–23; Galatians 3.26–end, 4.6–7; Luke 4.16–21

Men and women of learning

Proverbs 8.22–31; Ecclesiasticus 44.1–15
Psalms 36.5–10; 49.1–4
Philippians 4.7–8
Matthew 13.44–46, 52; John 7.14–18

Those whose holiness was revealed in marriage and family life

Proverbs 31.10–13, 19–20, 30–end; Tobit 8.4–7
Psalms 127; 128
I Peter 3.1–9
Mark 3.31–end; Luke 10.38–end

Mary Sumner (9 Aug): *also* Hebrews 13.1–5
Monica (27 Aug): *also* Ecclesiasticus 26.1–3, 13–16

¶ *Lectionary for Special Occasions*

The Guidance of the Holy Spirit

Proverbs 24.3–7; Isaiah 30.15–21; Wisdom 9.13–17
Psalms 25.1–9; 104.26–33; 143.8–10
Acts 15.23–29; Romans 8.22–27; 1 Corinthians 12.4–13
Luke 14.27–33; John 14.23–26; *or* 16.13–15

Rogation Days
(10–12 May in 2010)

Deuteronomy 8.1–10; 1 Kings 8.35–40; Job 28.1–11
Psalms 104.21–30; 107.1–9; 121
Philippians 4.4–7; 2 Thessalonians 3.6–13; 1 John 5.12–15
Matthew 6.1–15; Mark 11.22–24; Luke 11.5–13

Harvest Thanksgiving

Year A
Deuteronomy 8.7–18 *or* 28.1–14
Psalm 65
2 Corinthians 9.6–end
Luke 12.16–30 *or* 17.11–19

Year B
Joel 2.21–27
Psalm 126
1 Timothy 2.1–7 *or* 6.6–10
Matthew 6.25–33

Year C
Deuteronomy 26.1–11
Psalm 100
Philippians 4.4–9
or Revelation 14.14–18
John 6.25–35

Mission and Evangelism

Isaiah 49.1–6; *or* 52.7–10; Micah 4.1–5
Psalms 2; 46; 67
Acts 17.10–end; 2 Corinthians 5.14—6.2; Ephesians 2.13–end
Matthew 5.13–16; *or* 28.16–end; John 17.20–end

The Unity of the Church

Jeremiah 33.6–9*a*; Ezekiel 36.23–28; Zephaniah 3.16–end
Psalms 100; 122; 133
Ephesians 4.1–6; Colossians 3.9–17; 1 John 4.9–15
Matthew 18.19–22; John 11.45–52; *or* 17.11*b*–23

The Peace of the World

Isaiah 9.1–6; *or* 57.15–19; Micah 4.1–5
Psalms 40.14–17; 72.1–7; 85.8–13
Philippians 4.6–9; 1 Timothy 2.1–6; James 3.13–18
Matthew 5.43–end; John 14.23–29; *or* 15.9–17

Social Justice and Responsibility

Isaiah 32.15–end; Amos 5.21–24; *or* 8.4–7; Acts 5.1–11
Psalms 31.21–24; 85.1–7; 146.5–10
Colossians 3.12–15; James 2.1–4
Matthew 5.1–12; *or* 25.31–end; Luke 16.19–end

Ministry, including Ember Days

(See page 6)

Numbers 11.16–17, 24–29; *or* 27.15–end; 1 Samuel 16.1–13*a*; Isaiah 6.1–8; *or* 61.1–3; Jeremiah 1.4–10
Psalms 40.8–13; 84.8–12; 89.19–25; 101.1–5, 7; 122
Acts 20.28–35; 1 Corinthians 3.3–11; Ephesians 4.4–16; Philippians 3.7–14
Luke 4.16–21; *or* 12.35–43; *or* 22.24–27; John 4.31–38; *or* 15.5–17

In Time of Trouble

Genesis 9.8–17; Job 1.13–end; Isaiah 38.6–11
Psalms 86.1–7; 107.4–15; 142.1–7
Romans 3.21–26; Romans 8.18–25; 2 Corinthians 8.1–5, 9
Mark 4.35–end; Luke 12.1–7; John 16.31–end

For the Sovereign

Joshua 1.1–9; Proverbs 8.1–16
Psalms 20; 101; 121
Romans 13.1–10; Revelation 21.22—22.4
Matthew 22.16–22; Luke 22.24–30

The anniversary of HM The Queen's accession is 6 February.

Psalms in the Course of a Month

The following provision may be used for a monthly cycle of psalmody in place of the psalms provided in the tables in this booklet. It is based on the provision in The Book of Common Prayer.

	Morning Prayer	**Evening Prayer**
1	1—5	6—8
2	9—11	12—14
3	15—17	18
4	19—21	22—23
5	24—26	27—29
6	30—31	32—34
7	35—36	37
8	38—40	41—43
9	44—46	47—49
10	50—52	53—55
11	56—58	59—61
12	62—64	65—67
13	68	69—70
14	71—72	73—74
15	75—77	78
16	79—81	82—85
17	86—88	89
18	90—92	93—94
19	95—97	98—101
20	102—103	104
21	105	106
22	107	108—109
23	110—112	113—115
24	116—118	119.1–32
25	119.33–72	119.73–96
26	119.97–144	119.145–176
27	120—125	126—131
28	132—135	136—138
29	139—140	141—143
30	144—146	147—150

In February the psalms are read only to the 28th or 29th day of the month.

In January, March, May, July, August, October and December, all of which have 31 days, the same psalms are read on the last day of the month (being an ordinary weekday) which were read the day before, or else the psalms of the monthly course omitted on one of the Sundays in that month.

Concise Calendar November 2010 – December 2011

Advent 2010 to the eve of Advent 2011: Year A (Daily Eucharistic Lectionary Year 1)

November 2010

Sunday		3bAdv	2bAdv	ChrK	Adv1
Monday	**AllSS**	8	15	22	29
Tuesday	2	9	16	23	30
Wednesday	3	10	17	24	
Thursday	4	11	18	25	
Friday	5	12	19	26	
Saturday	6	13	20	27	

December 2010

Sunday		Adv2	Adv3	Adv4	Chr1
Monday		6	13	20	27
Tuesday		7	14	21	28
Wednesday	1	8	15	22	29
Thursday	2	9	16	23	30
Friday	3	10	17	24	31
Saturday	4	11	18	**Chr**	

January 2011

Sunday		Chr2	**Bapt**	Ep2	Ep3	Ep4
Monday		3	10	17	24	31
Tuesday		4	11	18	25	
Wednesday		5	12	19	26	
Thursday		**Ep**	13	20	27	
Friday		7	14	21	28	
Saturday	1	8	15	22	29	

February

Sunday		5bLnt	4bLnt	3bLnt	2bLnt
Monday		7	14	21	28
Tuesday	1	8	15	22	
Wednesday	**Pres**	9	16	23	
Thursday	3	10	17	24	
Friday	4	11	18	25	
Saturday	5	12	19	26	

March

Sunday		SbLnt	Lnt1	Lnt2	Lnt3
Monday		7	14	21	28
Tuesday	1	8	15	22	29
Wednesday	2	**Ash**	16	23	30
Thursday	3	10	17	24	31
Friday	4	11	18	**Ann**	
Saturday	5	12	19	26	

April

Sunday		Lnt4	Lnt5	PmS	**Est**
Monday		4	11	18	25
Tuesday		5	12	19	26
Wednesday		6	13	20	27
Thursday		7	14	**MTh**	28
Friday	1	8	15	**GFr**	29
Saturday	2	9	16	23	30

May

Sunday	Est2	Est3	Est4	Est5	Est6
Monday	2	9	16	23	30
Tuesday	3	10	17	24	31
Wednesday	4	11	18	25	
Thursday	5	12	19	26	
Friday	6	13	20	27	
Saturday	7	14	21	28	

June

Sunday		Est7	**Pent**	**TrS**	Tr1
Monday		6	13	20	27
Tuesday		7	14	21	28
Wednesday	1	8	15	22	29
Thursday	**Ascn**	9	16	23	30
Friday	3	10	17	24	
Saturday	4	11	18	25	

July

Sunday		Tr2	Tr3	Tr4	Tr5	Tr6
Monday		4	11	18	25	
Tuesday		5	12	19	26	
Wednesday		6	13	20	27	
Thursday		7	14	21	28	
Friday	1	8	15	22	29	
Saturday	2	9	16	23	30	

August

Sunday		Tr7	Tr8	Tr9	Tr10
Monday	1	8	15	22	29
Tuesday	2	9	16	23	30
Wednesday	3	10	17	24	31
Thursday	4	11	18	25	
Friday	5	12	19	26	
Saturday	6	13	20	27	

September

Sunday		Tr11	Tr12	Tr13	Tr14
Monday		5	12	19	26
Tuesday		6	13	20	27
Wednesday		7	14	21	28
Thursday	1	8	15	22	29
Friday	2	9	16	23	30
Saturday	3	10	17	24	

October

Sunday		Tr15	Tr16	Tr17	LaTr	4bAdv
Monday		3	10	17	24	31
Tuesday		4	11	18	25	
Wednesday		5	12	19	26	
Thursday		6	13	20	27	
Friday		7	14	21	28	
Saturday	1	8	15	22	29	

November 2011

Sunday		3bAdv	2bAdv	ChrK	Adv1
Monday		7	14	21	28
Tuesday	**AllSS**	8	15	22	29
Wednesday	2	9	16	23	30
Thursday	3	10	17	24	
Friday	4	11	18	25	
Saturday	5	12	19	26	

December 2011

Sunday		Adv2	Adv3	Adv4	**Chr**
Monday		5	12	19	26
Tuesday		6	13	20	27
Wednesday		7	14	21	28
Thursday	1	8	15	22	29
Friday	2	9	16	23	30
Saturday	3	10	17	24	31

On Sunday 26 December 2010 **Stephen, deacon, first martyr** may be celebrated.
On Sunday 30 January **The Presentation (Candlemas)**, transferred from 2 February, may be celebrated.
On Sunday 3 July **Thomas the Apostle** may be celebrated.
On Sunday 30 October **All Saints' Day**, transferred from 1 November, may be celebrated.